Magic at Midlife

Your Relationship Roadmap for Romance After 40

Jennifer Y. Levy-Peck, PhD

Charles Peck

Illustrations by
Lynda Louise Mangoro

HOPE THROUGH HEALING PUBLICATIONS

© 2016 Jennifer Y. Levy-Peck and Charles Peck

ISBN-10: 0-9743626-5-4
ISBN-13: 978-0-9743626-5-6

All rights reserved. Printed in the United States of America. No part of this publication may be reproduced, stored in a retrieval system, or transmitted in any form or by any means without the written permission of the publisher.

Publisher: Hope Through Healing Publications
P.O. Box 310
Yelm, WA 98597

Contents

ACKNOWLEDGEMENTS 1

INTRODUCTION: WHY YOU NEED A ROADMAP 3
   Is This Book for You? 4
   Where Do Roadmaps Come From? 5
   Sharing Travelers' Tales 6
   A Note on Pronouns 7
   Resources and References 7
   About Us 7

SECTION ONE: START YOUR ENGINE! 9
   CHAPTER 1: GET READY FOR THE ROAD 11
      Who Are You? 11
      Trace Your Relationship Route 13
      What's Your Bottom Line? 15
      Create a Vision of Your Future Life 16
      Set Your Own Goals 16
      Think About the Practical Issues 17
      Remember You Have Choices 18
   CHAPTER 2: BEFORE YOU SET OUT 21
      Are You Happy as a Single Person? 21
      Enjoying the Single Life 22
      Boost Your Health 24
      Tune Up Your Communication Skills 24
      Identify and Deal with Past Abuse .27
      Build Flexible Boundaries 28
      Strengthen Family Ties 29
      Sex the Way You Want It 29

SECTION TWO: FIND YOUR TRAVELING COMPANION 31
   CHAPTER 3: WHERE AND HOW TO LOOK 33
      Finding Your Special Someone 33
      Online Dating for the Older Set 36
      What You're Looking For 37
      Too Young or Too Old to Be Your Partner? 39
   CHAPTER 4: THE DATING GAME (IT'S DIFFERENT NOW) 41
      The First Date 41
      Who Pays for What on a Date? 41
      Falling in Love 43
      Timing Is Everything 44
      Older Hearts Break, Too 45

SECTION THREE: AM I ON THE RIGHT ROAD? 51

   CHAPTER 5: CAN I TRUST THIS PERSON? 53
      Sizing Up a Potential Partner 53
      Run, Don't Walk, to the Nearest Exit! 55
      Set Your Trust Meter 57
      Should You Do a Background Check? 60
      Privacy, Boundaries, and Trust 61

   CHAPTER 6: IS YOUR SWEETHEART A GROWN-UP? 63
      How Do You Measure Maturity? 63
      Work and Financial Stability 65
      Emotional Regulation and Stress Management 66
      Self-Reliance 68
      Relationships with Others 69
      Sense of Purpose and Achievement 70
      The 3 Cs: How to Know You've Found a Winner 70

   CHAPTER 7: WILL OUR LIVES FIT TOGETHER? 73
      Starting a New Relationship Before Your Kids Are Grown 73
      Consider Responsibilities for Aging Parents .75
      Fitting In with Friends 75
      Considering Religion and Spirituality 78
      Ten Questions to Deepen Your Relationship .78

SECTION FOUR: UPGRADE YOUR DRIVING SKILLS 81

   CHAPTER 8: COMMUNICATION 83
      Introvert or Extrovert? 83
      Keep Your Communication Skills in Tune 86
      Communication Basics 87
      Breaking the Silence 88

   CHAPTER 9: WHAT'S SEX GOT TO DO WITH IT? 91
      Midlife Sex: Complicated but Wonderful! 91
      To Do It or Not To Do It? 93
      What's Love Got to Do with It? 93
      How Do You Decide If It Is Time to Move Into a Sexual Relationship? 94
      Mature Adult Sex Ed 96
      Staying Healthy to Stay Sexy 98
      Dealing with Body Self-Consciousness 99
      Privacy and Other People – "Get a Room!" .100

   CHAPTER 10: LET'S TALK ABOUT SEX 103
      It's Good to Talk about Sex 103
      Having the "Senior Safer Sex" Conversation 105
      How Can You Talk about the Awkward Stuff? 106
      Trash from the Past (Childhood and Previous Relationships) 108
      Consent and Coercion 110
      Menopause and Sex 111
      Performance Issues 113
      Keeping Sex Special 115

CHAPTER 11: MAKING IT WORK 119
   Exploring New Roles Together 119
   Supporting Your Partner Emotionally 121
   Keep Unpacking Your Emotional Baggage 123

SECTION FIVE: ENJOY THE JOURNEY 125

CHAPTER 12: TERRITORY AND ROUTINES 127
   Your Place or Mine? Moving In Together 127
   Reimagining Your Life Together 128
   When One of You Retires 130

CHAPTER 13: THE "M" WORD – DO YOU WANNA GET MARRIED? 133
   To Marry or Not? 133
   Planning Your Wedding 134

CHAPTER 14: MONEY – IT'S HARDER TO TALK ABOUT THAN SEX! 137
   Money and Relationships 137
   Money – One Pot or Separate Accounts? 139
   Do You Need a Prenuptial Agreement? 141
   The Perils of Gift-Giving 141
   When You Need an Elder Law Attorney 143

CHAPTER 15: BLENDING FAMILIES – YOURS, MINE, AND OURS 145
   If You Still Have Kids at Home 145
   If Your Partner Has Kids at Home 146
   Helping Your Adult Children Accept Your New Partner 146
   Step-Grandparenting Can Be Grand 149
   Tending Your Relationship as You Tend to Aging Parents 150
   What About "The Ex"? 152
   Living with Pets 155

CHAPTER 16: IN SICKNESS AND IN HEALTH 157
   Encouraging Each Other Toward Wellness 157
   Sickness 159
   Memory Loss and Alzheimer's Disease 160
   Death 163

SECTION SIX: KEEP ON TRUCKIN' – AND SINGIN' TO THE RADIO 167

CHAPTER 17: PARTNERS ON THE ROAD 169
   Enjoy Your Stories 169
   Lucky to Have You: Gratitude Enhances Relationships 170

CHAPTER 18: KEEP YOUR SENSE OF HUMOR AND PLAYFULNESS 173
   Enjoy Life Together 173
   The Couple That Laughs Together, Stays Together 174

CHAPTER 19: SHARE YOUR HOPES AND DREAMS 177
   Creating Shared Goals 177
   Riding Through Life Together 178

RESOURCES AND REFERENCES 181
   Resources 181
   References 184

Acknowledgements

Many thanks to all the individuals and couples who shared their stories with us, particularly those who took the time to participate in our *Magic at Midlife* relationship survey. We appreciate your candor and have included your wisdom.

Thanks to our children (his and hers), their partners, and our grandchildren, who brighten our lives.

So many people have encouraged us to write this book, because they wanted guidance in their romantic journeys. We appreciate their support.

Michelle Roedell, editor of *Northwest Prime Time*, gave us a platform with our column in her newspaper and allowed us to publicize our relationship survey.

We were lucky to find two talented individuals to help us with this book: Lynda Louise Mangoro, our marvelous illustrator, and Sara Steinberg, our meticulous editor. The two of you helped to make our vision a reality.

Finally, we acknowledge each other, with love. Writing together has enhanced our journey.

Introduction: Why You Need a Roadmap

If you're over 40 and interested in a loving, long-lasting relationship, you may be wondering how you will be able to find the right partner or how to sustain a healthy and happy romantic partnership. Perhaps your heart is dented and scratched a bit from previous experiences, or maybe it is a little dusty and rusty from sitting in the driveway for some time. But a lifetime is a long time, and you know it can be a lonely road to travel by yourself. So how do you reach your destination of becoming part of a happy twosome—and enjoying the journey along the way?

Jennifer, one of the authors of this book, was widowed at age 50 after 31 years of marriage. The last time she had dated someone other than her first husband was when she was 15 years old. Charles, the other author, emerged from more than two decades of marriage without a clear sense of how to go about finding a true partner, and leaped a little too fast into an "oops" marriage that lasted a very short time. We found each other online through a matchmaking website that required an investment of time, energy, and thoughtfulness; two years later, we married. As we spoke to friends and acquaintances about our experiences, many of them confessed to the same confusion, insecurity, and just plain ignorance that the two of us felt in our quest for true love.

The dating world had changed significantly since Jennifer was a teenager and Charles was a young bachelor. Jennifer couldn't put on her bell-bottom jeans and tie-dyed T-shirt and head for the discotheque; the Air Force uniform Charles wore on his early dates was boxed up in his closet, musty and a bit too tight. We both had questions and concerns, and weren't sure where to turn for the answers. How could we protect our hearts and keep ourselves safe while searching for "the one"? What did "dating" even look like for middle-aged people with adult children, mortgages, demanding jobs, health issues, a few wrinkles, an aging parent, two dogs and two cats?

While no one can tell you who will be right for you, or exactly what you should do in any given circumstance, it helps to have a roadmap that identifies the questions you should be asking yourself as you travel this route, points out possible deep mud puddles or dangerous cliffs, and helps you to envision what to expect. *Magic at Midlife* advises you on how to equip yourself for the journey, what to pack and what to jettison, and how to keep on truckin' down the highway of happiness once you have found your special someone. Whether you are a man or a woman, 45 or 75, you deserve love and you can learn how to create a strong and lasting relationship.

Is This Book for You?

This book was written for people 40 and above (with no upper age limit) who are considering a long-term, committed, monogamous relationship or who are interested in understanding and improving their current relationship. It doesn't matter whether you're with an opposite-sex or same-sex partner, whether you are 45 or 85, whether marriage is in the picture or not, or whether you've previously had dozens of partners or none at all.

When we began doing research for this book, we conducted a survey of midlife adults. One respondent scolded us for not addressing polyamorous relationships – that is, relationships among several people at once. As far as we're concerned, consenting adults can do what they want as long as they are not harming others, but polyamorous relationships and hookups for sex alone are outside the scope of this book.

That said, you may not be sure that a committed relationship is right for you at this point in your life. We'll help you to explore that question, and it's okay if you decide that you don't want to go down that road.

We do want to acknowledge that we couldn't cover everything. For example, we realize that not everyone identifies as a man or a woman – there's a whole range of gender identities and expressions. We still use the terms "men" and "women" in this book because that is how most people identify, and while trans people will find some universal truths in this book, it may not be tailored for their specific needs and issues. We did try to be inclusive of same-sex relationships, but there may be some sections that are more relevant to those in heterosexual partnerships.

We want to give you a roadmap for the entire journey, from finding your sweetheart to sustaining a wonderful relationship. The decisions are yours; we simply provide you with a clear picture of the landscape.

Where Do Roadmaps Come From?

When we set out to write our book on midlife relationships, we hit upon the idea of a "relationship roadmap" because it seemed that midlife relationships are sometimes hard to navigate. The truth is, we all have our own internal relationship roadmaps, based on our past experiences and beliefs, and some of them lead to destinations we don't want to visit!

Our parents or other adults in our household gave us our first set of directions for relationships. Think about this. What did you learn while growing up, and from whom? What we observe about how parents, stepparents, or other adults in our families treat one another makes a huge difference in what we expect for our own relationships. Charles and Jennifer had very different experiences growing up. In his household, he witnessed very little open affection and no one talked about how partners should relate to each other. Jennifer's parents adored each other and were openly affectionate and loving. This created different sets of expectations that we had to learn to explain to one another.

The next set of "driving instructions" we receive comes from our dating and marriage experiences early in life. We learn to behave a certain way within a relationship, partly in response to how the other person acts. For example, if our partner turns out to be harsh when angry, we may learn to avoid conflict and keep our opinions to ourselves. This pattern can continue into later relationships, where it can make it hard to be open and emotionally close to a partner, even a loving one.

We also pick up a set of directions and other messages from the media and society. Many of us came of age in the 1960s and '70s, when roles were changing rapidly for men and women, same-sex relationships were finally out in the open, and sexuality became a topic of conversation. We received mixed messages about who we should be and how we should act in relationships. All this was exhilarating, but confusing at times.

Fortunately, most of us have the capacity to draw our own relationship roadmaps. You can decide what you want in a partner, how you want to interact, and what you consider healthy and worthwhile. If you can identify and acknowledge the directions you were given in the past, you can change them, if that's what you want to do. As you get to know a potential partner, you'll want to describe your vision of the road ahead, and ask for theirs. You and your partner are continuously creating your journey together.

Sharing Travelers' Tales

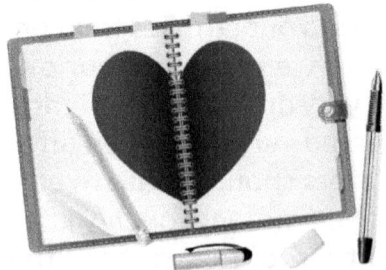

Throughout this book, we have shared what we call "Travelers' Tales." These are stories based upon what we have been told by friends, people we have met in our professional lives, and individuals who were kind enough to take our informal *Magic at Midlife*

survey, which they learned of through social media and the column we wrote for *Northwest Prime Time*. We have taken care to remove any personally identifying information, and some of the stories are composites. All names have been changed, except in those cases where we describe our own experiences. We appreciate people's willingness to share their tales in hope of helping others.

A Note on Pronouns

Because it is awkward to repeat "his or her," and because we want this book to be as gender-inclusive as possible, we have chosen to use the singular "they." This usage is becoming more accepted and reflects the way most of us speak.

Resources and References

At the end of this book, you will find reference information for research that is cited as well as a list of helpful resources on various topics.

About Us

Charles Peck is the former co-author (with Jennifer) of the column "Magic at Midlife" in *Northwest Prime Time*. His professional career has included everything from innovative carpentry to computer network administration. He has also worked as a professional editor.

Jennifer Y. Levy-Peck, PhD, is a licensed psychologist and has her own human services firm, Levy-Peck Consulting, LLC. She provides evaluation, training, and technical writing related to victim advocacy and related topics. Jennifer worked as a therapist, focusing on trauma survivors, for more than 30 years. Her practice included couples and family therapy. She earned her PhD in Clinical Psychology at George Washington University in

Washington, DC. She has written a book for parents of children who have been sexually abused, and has co-edited and contributed to two volumes on intimate partner sexual violence.

Jennifer and Charles live among the evergreens in Washington State.

SECTION ONE: START YOUR ENGINE!

It takes courage to grow up and become who you really are.
—e.e. cummings, poet

SECTION ONE:
START YOUR ENGINE!

Chapter 1: Get Ready for the Road

> No matter what you do,
> you'll never run away from you.
> –Paul Revere and the Raiders, "Kicks"

Who Are You?

Many people experience a profound sense of dislocation in middle age, particularly if they lose a long-term partnership to death, divorce, or separation. For years, they were part of a "we"; now they are simply an "I." When you face the world solo, things look different. You may have lost track of who you truly are. In a relationship, we compromise and accommodate, and we are changed in the process. As an individual, you may have to reestablish your own identity. What do you like to do? What options are available to you? Something as simple as figuring out what you would like to have for dinner may be difficult after many years of eating a certain way because of your partner's preferences.

You can't connect effectively in a relationship unless you are willing to invest some time in discovering who you are at this point in your life. This is a good time to write in a journal or use some other creative medium to explore your thoughts, your feelings, your values, and your desires. What is important to you?

TRAVELERS' TALES

Jan was married for 25 years to Tony, and she spent a lot of her energy trying to please him. A handsome and charismatic man, he was moody and self-centered. Jan gave up many of the things she liked to do because it was a hassle to argue with Tony; he punished her by being withdrawn or irritable if she disagreed with him. When Tony ended the marriage abruptly, explaining that he was involved with another woman and wanted to be with her, Jan went through a period of profound sadness and self-doubt. As she began to recover and feel better about herself, she realized that she really didn't know herself any more. She had been caught up with work, raising kids, and catering to Tony for so long that she was unsure what to do with her time and energy. Gradually, she began exploring new interests and activities. Jan found that she could create a satisfying life that reflected *her* tastes and wishes—once she knew what they were.

If you don't like the person you are, work to make any needed changes before setting out to find a partner. You don't have to be perfect, but you do want to be self-confident and reasonably happy with yourself. If you're anxious about how you look, decide what you can realistically change, and figure out how to be comfortable with the rest. If you don't see yourself as interesting, get out and do something you might like, just as Jan did in the story above. To boost your confidence, think about why your friends like you. Are you a caring person? Do you follow through on your promises? Do you have a loving heart? These qualities will make you a terrific partner for some lucky person.

> ### SET YOUR DIRECTION
>
> Take a bit of time to get to know yourself a little better. Write a few sentences describing someone you admire greatly. Go back and circle the words that describe this person. How many of these words describe you as well? You may not be able to become a second John Lennon or Oprah Winfrey, but you can cultivate in yourself the qualities you admire in your idols. If you value creativity or compassion or trustworthiness or assertiveness, what can you do to increase these aspects of your own personality?

Trace Your Relationship Route

Most of us begin to think about what we want in a relationship when we start dating (or thinking about it) as teens. There's just one problem with this: the portions of our brain that are involved in rational decision-making are not fully formed in our youth. Teenagers are more impulsive, more easily stirred by emotions, and less able to apply good judgment to emotionally charged situations than adults. The experiences and expectations of adolescence can shape our ideas about what a relationship should be like, so it's worth a look backward before we begin to consider a midlife relationship.

Think about the pattern of your previous relationships. Be aware that we all develop "stories" about our life that help us to justify our actions and, often, to put the blame on others when things go wrong. If you really want to learn from your past, this portion of your journey will probably be somewhat difficult and painful. You have to be completely honest with yourself, and focus on identifying your own behaviors and mistakes in past relationships. It doesn't do any good to blame past partners. Don't blame yourself, either, because blame doesn't move you forward in life. Do, however, try to identify any of your own beliefs and behaviors that have interfered with the quality of your past relationships.

You need some quiet time to reflect on these issues. Reflection comes easily to some people, while others may find it more of a challenge. In any case, use the tools that help you most. You may find that writing is a great way to sort out your feelings; many people use a journal (paper or online) for this purpose.

Be cautious about sharing your journal and protecting your privacy, because this part of your journey should be for you alone. Writing for an audience changes the nature of the task. You may also regret sharing your innermost thoughts before they are fully formed. If you prefer to think things through with someone else, choose a trusted friend or a therapist. You need to create a peaceful, private environment to think about your life and relationships.

These questions can guide you as you consider each past relationship:

1. How well did I know myself before I started this relationship?
2. How well did I know my partner?
3. What surprised me the most as this relationship developed?
4. Looking back, were there hints of trouble ahead?
5. Why did I miss those hints?
6. What were the good and bad aspects of each relationship?
7. How have my needs changed over the years?
8. What pain am I still carrying from the past?
9. What behaviors and beliefs do I need to change so I can

participate in a healthy relationship?
10. What information and support do I need, and how can I find it?

Be particularly careful, as you go through this process, to avoid blaming yourself for:

- ignorance – we're all ignorant until we learn something!
- victimization – it's not your fault if you were abused in any way.

You can take responsibility for your errors without beating yourself up emotionally. Everyone makes mistakes, and we are not born knowing how to have healthy relationships. Unless you were lucky enough to have a great relationship model in your family while growing up, you have to develop your own guidelines for what you want and then learn how to shape your future.

If this process is unbearably painful, this indicates the need to spend more time dealing with how your past is still alive in the present. Therapy or a support group may help you to put the past in the past, and to move forward toward a happier future. Some people get stuck on their anger and bitterness, while others pretend (even to themselves) that everything is perfect. Neither extreme is workable. Everything that has happened has made you into the person you are today, and offers an opportunity for learning and growth.

What's Your Bottom Line?

It's critical to think about what you really must have in a relationship and what you truly can't put up with, as you begin thinking about finding someone to share your life. For example, if you can't stand the thought of being with a racist individual in the long term, don't waste your time with an amusing bigot. We each have some core beliefs and values that are the bedrock for any relationship. What are yours?

Write a few sentences for yourself in response to these prompts:

I could NOT be with someone with these qualities:

The person I am with MUST have these qualities:

Don't let anyone tell you that you're being too picky when you insist on these core qualities. On the other hand, think hard about what your core values truly are. You may find yourself attracted to someone who looks different than your image of an ideal mate. That's great, but if you find yourself interested in a person who violates your fundamental standards (for example, someone who treats children poorly), think twice (or 12 times!).

Create a Vision of Your Future Life

Before she met Charles, Jennifer went on one date with a perfectly nice man who retired early so he could ride his motorcycle wherever his fancy took him. Jennifer is too much of a chicken to ride a motorcycle, likes home life, has ties to family, and is still working full time. Motorcycle Man was not exactly a match made in heaven.

Set Your Own Goals

In midlife and beyond, we realize that our time on Earth is not infinite, and we focus more on what we want to accomplish while we're still here. This awareness is also helpful as you ponder a potential relationship or seek to enhance your present one. If what you want more than anything is to spend quality time with your young grandchildren and to be an important influence in their lives, you're not going to be very happy with a person who doesn't enjoy the company of children. If your goal is to travel around the globe, a homebody is probably not the best match for you. Sometimes couples will work together on joint goals, and this can be exciting; at other times you may want the space and support to do your own thing without worrying that it is eroding your relationship.

> What are your three top short-term goals (for the next two years)?
> 1.
> 2.
> 3.
>
> What are your three most important long-term goals (what you want to accomplish before you die, not to be morbid or anything)?
> 1.
> 2.
> 3.
>
> What would you need from a partner to help you reach these goals?

If you are in the beginning stages of a relationship, be sure to ask your prospective partner about goals, dreams, and priorities in life. Pay close attention to whether a potential partner is truly interested in what you want in the long run, and see whether your goals mesh or complement each other. If you choose to stay together, you want your long-term goals to be in harmony.

Think About the Practical Issues

Before you begin to envision a future partner, consider some of the practical issues that may be important to you in the future.

If marriage is critical to you, be clear about that from the beginning. Some people past the age of 40 have no desire whatsoever to get married or to remarry. Online dating can make broaching this delicate subject early in the relationship a bit easier, because it's often one of the questions you'll be asked by the dating program, to establish compatibility. Certainly it would be awkward to announce on a first date, "I am looking for a wife (or a husband)!" Nonetheless, it helps to know from the beginning whether marriage is on the table, whether you are seeking wedded bliss or running as fast as you can away from the idea of matrimony.

Later in this book, we discuss in detail merging a new partnership with one's existing family relationships and responsibilities, whether they involve aging parents, children still at home, adult children, or grandchildren (and even pets!). At this point, you just want to think through the shape of your life and what role you expect a partner to play. While your priorities and lifestyle may shift as you build a committed relationship, there may be some nonnegotiable issues that must be considered up front, such as your role in the care of a disabled adult child. If you are just dating to have fun, it isn't so critical to consider these issues, but if you're looking for a lifetime partner, you can't avoid focusing on how your needs and goals will match up.

Remember You Have Choices

It is your choice whether to look for lasting love and how you want to construct a relationship. This is one of the true joys of our stage in life. To stay single or to see people casually is perfectly okay, if that's what you want. You can enter into a very traditional mom-and-pop (or grandma-and-grandpa) relationship, or you can live on opposite coasts of the country and see each other twice a month. You don't have to buy into any stereotypes of what your relationship should be. Perhaps you were in a heterosexual marriage earlier in life, but you realized that wasn't for you, and you now seek a same-sex relationship. It's no one's business but yours if you want a younger partner, an older partner, a partner of a different race or ethnicity, or someone very different from the rest of your family in some other way. The choice is yours.

TRAVELERS' TALES

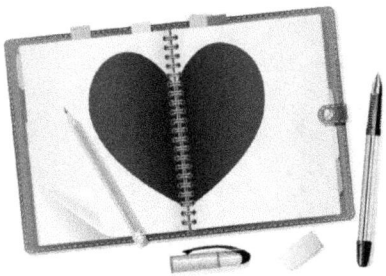

Shirley was in her early sixties when her husband Frank died. Frank was a character – well known and respected in their small rural town. However, he treated Shirley with a complete lack of respect. He was controlling and often told her that she was stupid and was doing things wrong. Shirley loved Frank, but she was resentful of his put-downs and tired of having to cater to his whims. A couple of years after his death, she became reacquainted with Jim, a local man in his mid-forties who seemed much more carefree. Jim rode a motorcycle and didn't take life too seriously. Shirley was a trim and attractive woman who didn't look her age, and she and Jim became friends. To her surprise, Shirley found that she loved riding on Jim's motorcycle and being with someone who didn't order her around. Jim appreciated Shirley's kindness toward his mother, who was ill, and they shared a sense of humor. Shirley changed her matronly hairdo for long, curly highlights and bought herself a leather jacket. Tongues were wagging in their little town, but to her surprise, Shirley found she just didn't care. She had spent 40 years taking good care of Frank, despite his crankiness, and she decided that if being with Jim made her feel good, she was going to ignore the gossip and follow her heart.

Chapter 2: Before You Set Out

> We can walk our road together if our goals are all the same.
> We can run alone and free if we pursue a different aim.
> –Rush, *Hemispheres*, "VI. The Sphere"

Are You Happy as a Single Person?

It seems rather strange that one of the best ways to prepare for a relationship is to make sure you are happy while you're single, but it's true. You can't count on someone else to fill in the gaps if you don't have a satisfying life. By focusing on creating an enjoyable, self-sufficient life for yourself, you make it more likely that a healthy, mature partner will want to join you. If you are waiting for Prince or Princess Charming to solve your financial problems, keep you from being bored, fix everything in your life that needs fixing, and be your entire social circle, you're setting yourself up for an unbalanced relationship. If you don't function well on your own, you may attract a controlling or parental individual as a "partner." These relationships tend to break down when the needy partner gains strength.

Of course, the right partner will enhance your life and help you to be an even better person and to have more strength and pleasure in your life. But until your traveling partner comes along, embark on your own journey to make your life better every day.

Here are some ways you can make your single life more fulfilling:

- Find something new that you really love doing, whether it is salsa dancing, volunteering at a school, learning a new language, or adopting a rescue pet.
- Get your financial house in order, to the best of your ability (see Chapters 12 and 14).
- Focus on your friendships. Work on being the very best friend you can be – those skills are similar to the ones that

make relationships successful.
- Don't be afraid to do things alone, or to invite a friend. If you want to go out to the movies, museums, or a restaurant, do it!
- Stay physically active as much as possible. This will enhance your mood and make you feel better about yourself.
- Make sure you are balancing your own needs with those of your friends and family. If you feel chronically resentful and "put-upon," you're not taking good care of yourself.
- Spend time with good people – optimistic and supportive folks who genuinely care about you. You will be vulnerable to poor relationship decision-making if you feel unappreciated and lonely.

Enjoying the Single Life

Since the title of this book is *Magic at Midlife*, it's probably obvious that we believe in joyous relationships. Yet we also realize that "couplehood," like parenthood, is not for everyone. Some people choose to be single, and we celebrate that choice. Have 12 lovers or none - it's your life, and you alone can make those decisions for yourself.

Even those who would prefer to have a partner are likely to spend part of their later years alone. After all, a substantial number of marriages or partnerships end in divorce or separation, and in lasting couples, one partner will likely outlive the other. If you're newly single, for whatever reason, it will take some getting used to. How you approach your single state will make a big difference in the quality of your life.

First, don't buy into the stereotypes. Why are single women regarded as lonely spinsters to be pitied, while single men are seen as playboys to be envied? Neither view is accurate in most cases. There's a lot of social pressure to be part of a couple, so speak up if you feel your decisions are not being respected.

Make your life full, not empty. Think about what you want, what fulfills you, and what makes you feel productive. Then do it. Go back to school, take up whale watching, or refinish a chair. Stay happily busy and engaged in life.

Make your house a home. Just because you live by yourself, you don't need to eat off a tray or live out of boxes. Make your "nest" your own special haven and a welcoming spot where you can invite friends.

Consider a pet. It's much less lonely to come home to a tail-wagging, purring, or chirping fan than to an empty house. A word to the wise: You may not want to let your dog or cat get used to sleeping in the bed with you if you want a sex life in the future. It's hard to focus when your pooch is snarling at your lover or your cat is scratching at the bedroom door. Just saying.

Find friends. Join a walking club, a book club, or an environmental group. Get politically active. Use a site such as www.meetup.com to find people who are interested in common activities and friendship. Learn to play bridge or join a community chorus. Discover what level of social activity suits you—not too much, not too little.

Don't put off what you want to do. If you want to travel, travel (find a tour for mature singles if you don't want to go by yourself). If you want to see a movie, buy yourself some popcorn and enjoy. Take a book to a restaurant if you wish, or just relax alone. Don't worry what others may think. They are probably not thinking about you at all (they are busy checking their own text messages)!

Just say no. If you feel you are being pressured to consider a relationship and you don't want it, remember it is your choice – not your children's, your mother's, or your Great Aunt Sue's. If you have been widowed or divorced, you will heal in your own time, not when others think you should.

Be clear about your intentions. If you want to date but don't want a committed relationship, say so at the start. Be wary of potential partners who think they will rescue you from loneliness or convince you to get married. Find someone whose goals match your own.

Have fun! Spend the weekend in your pajamas, eat what you want when you want it, go to bed late or get up early, and enjoy the perks of being on your own. Whether or not you want a relationship eventually, you'll be an interesting person with a satisfying life.

Boost Your Health

The older we get, the more challenging it becomes to maintain good health. If you want to be able to enjoy a relationship, including a sexual relationship, good health is a plus. You may have chronic health conditions that you can't control, but lifestyle choices are some of the most important factors in long-term health.

Try to find an activity you enjoy such as walking, water aerobics, or bicycling. This has to be something you can do on a regular basis. Research shows that an exercise partner can help you to stay motivated (remember, your dog can be your walking partner!). If you've been fairly inactive or have physical limitations, start slowly and consider getting expert advice from a physician, personal trainer, or physical therapist.

Don't ignore chronic health problems that are affecting your life. While your future partner should be supportive and helpful whatever happens, it is only fair that you work on your own health to the extent possible.

Tune Up Your Communication Skills

Good communication skills are so very important in creating and maintaining a healthy relationship. Most of us could use a "tune-up" on these skills.

Take the following quiz to assess your communication skills:

1. I usually "go along to get along" and don't speak up about my needs or preferences.*
2. I am easily irritated and sometimes fly off the handle.*
3. If something bothers me, I try to talk about it calmly.
4. I often find myself doing things I really don't want to do, because I haven't said "no."*
5. I tend to press others to go along with my ideas.*
6. I've been told that I am bossy or critical.*
7. I like it when someone else makes most of the decisions.*
8. I want to make my opinions known, but I like to hear others' thoughts as well.
9. I often agree just to avoid an argument, and then I do whatever I want (sometimes by hiding what I do).*
10. It scares me when people argue, even if they are not really fighting.*
11. I like to argue for the sake of arguing.*
12. I can stand up for myself without being hateful.
13. I get along well with most people.
14. I often regret the way I talk to others when I am angry.*
15. In a previous relationship, I forced my partner to do things (verbally or physically).*
16. In a previous relationship, I was forced to do things (verbally or physically).*
17. I am estranged from more than one person who used to be in my life (other than a former partner).*
18. I have good relationships with almost all of my family members.
19. I am willing to apologize and take responsibility for my behavior.
20. I am sad or angry much of the time.*

Take a good look at the items with an asterisk (*). These are behaviors or experiences that can lead to communication and relationship problems.

If you typically don't speak up, don't express your preferences or opinions, and expect others to make all the decisions, you're demonstrating what we call *passive* behavior. Often people who have grown up in homes with a great deal of conflict prefer to avoid any conflict at all, so they use a passive style. These people are often described as "nice" or "sweet," but underneath the niceness, like the pool of molten rock under a dormant volcano, there may be a reservoir of unexpressed anger or resentment. If you don't show that you respect your own needs, you're likely to wind up with a partner who doesn't respect them either – and that can feel awful. The passive style works in the short term, because it helps you to avoid overt disagreement, but ultimately you feel worse and worse about yourself if you aren't able to make your needs known. In our society, women are often expected to behave in this way, but it leads to frustration and an unbalanced, unequal relationship that benefits no one. Men certainly use these strategies as well.

If you tend to become angry or irritated with little provocation, and you push your views onto others, you are using an *aggressive* communication style. Again, this way of handling conflict can work in the short term, because you may be able to intimidate others into complying with your desires. You pay a huge price, though. Other people don't like aggressive individuals very much. You push them away, because they can't trust you enough to be vulnerable. You also set up a situation where your partner is liable to lie to you or go behind your back, because you don't make it easy to have an open and honest conversation. If you really want a genuine partnership and emotional closeness, you'll have to find a different way of relating.

If you can usually stand up for yourself, speak clearly about things that bother you, identify and express your own needs, and treat others with respect, you're fortunate enough to be an *assertive* person. These are skills that can be learned, even in midlife. Assertive individuals are more likely to attract others with similar communication styles, and to have the skills to build a healthy and mutually respectful relationship.

Identify and Deal with Past Abuse

If you've been on either end of an abusive relationship in the past, you MUST deal with this before you try to find another partner. Abuse takes many forms. It can be verbal and emotional, with frequent put-downs and belittling of the other person. It can be physical. Many people fail to identify physical abuse. They say, "Well, he (or she) never actually hit me." Pushing, shoving, strangling, and using physical size or force to intimidate another person *is* abusive. Sexual abuse and coercion also often go unrecognized in relationships. Marriage or living together is not a "blank check" for sexual activity. Each sexual encounter requires active consent by both partners. If you've pressured a partner to do something sexually that the person didn't enjoy, or if you have complied with sex because you were afraid of what would happen if you didn't, you have been in a sexually abusive relationship.

Whether emotional, physical, or sexual, all abuse is intended as a way to control another person. This control damages individuals, families, and relationships. You deserve better, if you have been abused. If you were the one trying to establish control, you know this pattern of behavior was destructive and did not result in the type of relationship you truly wanted.

What can you do about a history of abuse in an intimate relationship? In addition to soul-searching and being as honest as you can with yourself, there is help available. If you were the one who exerted power and control, seek a therapist who is experienced in working with these issues and take whatever time you need to work through these concerns. You need to identify your own behavior patterns and learn new ways to cope with conflict in a healthier manner.

If you've been on the receiving end of any form of abuse, you need support as well. Even if the abuse was years in the past, therapy may be helpful, and you may also wish to consider receiving advocacy services. Advocacy agencies (often called domestic violence or sexual assault programs) usually offer free, confidential support. These programs provide individual help as well as support groups for survivors of abuse to learn about what happened to them and find ways of building their skills and self-esteem so they can recover and thrive. It was not your fault if you were abused, and investing in your own recovery will make it much more likely that you can participate in a healthy relationship in the future.

The Resources section at the end of this book contains information about organizations that provide free, confidential help with issues of domestic or sexual violence.

Build Flexible Boundaries

Healthy boundaries are the hallmark of a healthy relationship. They are the limits that you set based on self-knowledge and self-respect. If your annoying neighbor drops by several times a day without calling, your adult kids expect you to wash their dirty clothes, your co-workers take advantage of your good nature, or your mom still treats you as if you were 10 years old, you need to work on building and maintaining clearer and stronger boundaries.

On the other hand, if you isolate yourself, can't trust people even after they have proven themselves trustworthy, find it hard to reach out to those in need, or push away people you'd like to know better, your boundaries have hardened into impenetrable walls. Think of boundaries as being like a burglar alarm system. You don't want the alarm to go off every time a squirrel runs into your yard, but you also don't want to give out the code to everyone you know. Just the right degree of sensitivity and protection is what keeps you safe while staying connected to the outside world.

Working on your communication skills and boundary issues before you search for a sweetheart can pay big dividends. You are more likely to find a partner whose own boundaries are flexible yet strong, and you'll know how to expect respect.

Strengthen Family Ties

Before you embark on a quest for a romantic relationship, pay attention to the other relationships you have within your family. For example, Brian divorced after a very brief marriage, because his wife was completely enmeshed with her mother and wasn't emotionally free to be his partner. If you are estranged from one of your children or have been neglecting a sibling or grandchild, do what you can to repair the relationship (unless you have been abused by that person).

If things aren't going well between you and a family member, this has the potential to disrupt a future partnership. You can't fix everything, but if improving a family relationship is within your control, you may be able to pave the way for a more drama-free future with a partner.

Sex the Way *You* Want It

Let's face it, it's a little funny that we have to deal with the same issues in midlife as we did in our teens and young adult years. How did you handle sexuality in your early dating life? What factors went into your decisions about whether to be sexually active, your choices about contraception, and your views about when it was appropriate to include sexual behaviors in your relationships? Probably your parents' guidelines influenced you (possibly to do the exact opposite of what they wished), along with the peer culture in which you grew up, your religious or cultural beliefs, and your gender.

Before you set out to find a romantic connection, it is worth re-evaluating your sexual values. Are you comfortable with casual sex? Do you want to reserve physical intimacy for an emotionally intimate relationship? We do talk about sex throughout this book, and we encourage readers to engage their heads as well as their hearts and their bodies in sexual decision-making. At this point in your journey, give some thought to what a satisfying sexual relationship would look like for you, and how important an active sex life is for you. There are no right or wrong answers, but this is the time to reflect on your own wishes.

SECTION TWO: FIND YOUR TRAVELING COMPANION

Chapter 3: Where and How to Look

> Hold the line, love isn't always on time.
> –Toto, "Hold the Line"

Finding Your Special Someone

It can be daunting to venture out into the "mature" dating world. How can you find a partner? Where should you begin?

Be firm. Be clear with yourself about your bottom-line issues, and then hold fast. Don't compromise on something essential just to avoid being alone. Know the red flags for destructive relationships (see Chapter 5) and run, don't walk, to the nearest exit if those flags are flying.

Be flexible. Beyond the essentials, be open-minded about how you might find a partner and what that person may look like. You can be creative in your search, and if you are open about the non-essentials, you may have some wonderful surprises. Perhaps you thought online dating was just for losers, but now it is one of the most popular ways to find a mate (that's how we met each other, and how several people who took our relationship survey met their partners). Maybe you have a mental image of your ideal partner that doesn't take into account how attractive the right person can become to you, regardless of their physical appearance.

Be friendly. A smile will draw people to you, or at the very least, it will make you feel better! You might meet a potential partner where you least expect to, such as the dentist's office or the driver's license bureau, if you're willing to smile and make friendly conversation. Also consider that people who aren't potential partners have a social network that might include just the right person for you – so be nice to everyone!

Be fun-loving. It's amazing how attractive people who are enjoying themselves can be. Seek out activities that you really enjoy, and you're likely to find someone who shares your interests and tastes. There is an online group, a club, or a meeting place for just about every interest under the sun. Take some time to consider what is truly fun for you.

Be flirty. If your flirting skills are rusty, get back in practice. Be brave enough to approach someone who interests you. You can start with friendship and see where things develop from there. Some people who responded to our relationship survey said they had reconnected with old friends and romance had blossomed.

Be fascinated. Have you always wanted to take up skydiving or salsa dancing? Now's the time to step out and try new things. Volunteer at a local agency, attend a professional conference (even if you're retired), or take a class. You'll meet people this way, and they are likely to be interesting to you. It's also less awkward to get to know someone if you are both focused on a task or an activity.

Be frank. At this point in life, you should have a pretty good idea of who you are and what you want. Don't waste time by being anything less than authentic. Be honest and clear in your communication as you get to know a potential partner, and you'll be more likely to find someone who thinks you are special.

TRAVELERS' TALES

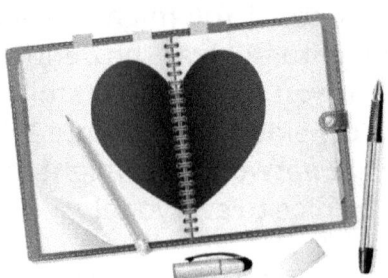

According to our informal *Magic at Midlife* survey,

respondents met their special someone in a variety of ways. Here are some of their responses:

"In a choir. I think people need to try different social activities as much for self-fulfillment as for meeting more people."

"We met through an online dating site." [Several couples met this way.]

"Friends set us up. It was a surprise." [Several couples met through friends.]

"Work."

"Married my brother's best friend."

"I finally connected with my partner after admiring him from afar for five years. I had a crush on him from the first time I saw him. Funny how right one's instincts can be! However, we both were in other relationships. After five years finally the stars aligned and I was able to have a date with him – I was like a nervous teenager all over again. Fantastic!"

"We met through family activities. Although no one intended to bring the two of us together, we discovered each other at a family gathering."

"Knew each other in high school; ran into each other at a restaurant."

"We met in high school, finally got married 20 years later. Tip: Do NOT look for mates in bars!"

"Parents Without Partners."

"I met my partner in a running club – we both ran together with mutual friends."

Online Dating for the Older Set

We met online. Jennifer was living in a rural college town and found the pool of eligible men to be, shall we say, pretty shallow. Charles liked the idea of getting well acquainted with a woman before starting to date. Accordingly, each of us found our way to eHarmony.com and began filling out the lengthy questionnaires required by that site. One survey asked about "Must Haves" and "Can't Stands." For example, "I must have a partner who is honest and reliable." "I can't stand people who are racist." When Jennifer saw Charles's answers to these questions, she thought she was looking at her own responses. Ah, Fate!

Even so, Jennifer almost ruled Charles out as a dating partner at first because of the seven-year age difference. Charles almost ignored Jennifer's listing because she lived about 310 miles from him, whereas he had chosen a 300-mile radius for his search. Yet somehow we connected.

Over the next several weeks, we corresponded intensely. At first, we did so through the dating site, allowing us to get acquainted without having to share identifying information. Soon we exchanged email addresses, and delved into an all-consuming online correspondence, feeling as though we were both teenagers again (Jennifer was 53 and Charles was 60 at the time). We had each decided that we would lay our cards on the table, sharing as much information as possible in the attempt to find someone who would accept us completely.

Above all, we chose to spend several weeks getting to know each other online before we (with hearts pounding!) met in person. Later, we both felt that connecting online was a priceless opportunity to communicate about what really mattered, without the distraction of being physically together. We talked about our previous relationships, our families, our values, our hopes, our fears, the good and bad choices we had made in life, and the things that made us smile. We went through the work day with our minds on the evening, when each of us would find a lengthy message waiting, to our delight. After a few weeks, we planned a phone call. It was such a thrill to hear each other's voices for the first time!

How did we come to know that our potential partner was "the real deal"? We weren't naïve; we know that many people lie online. In fact, one study showed that about half of online daters lie about their height and weight, and about 20 percent lie about their age – not by much, but they do lie. Jennifer's friends, in particular, were concerned about her safety and whether she could trust the information that Charles was giving her. Like many online daters, Jennifer searched the internet for information about Charles. Moreover, she examined his correspondence for consistency and emotional authenticity, as Charles did with her communications. We asked a lot of questions and made note of the other's willingness to answer fully and deeply. Charles expressed his wish for Jennifer to feel safe in the budding relationship; he offered to wait before meeting, provide any personal information she might like, and to take gradual steps in building the relationship.

About 17 percent of Americans who were married in 2015 met their spouse online. Nearly 21 percent of the over-forties in our (interesting but unscientific) relationship study met their partners online. We are not recommending specific dating sites because these change so quickly. Instead, we suggest that you talk to friends and read articles from reputable sources such as AARP before choosing a dating site. We know from personal experience that, with appropriate caution, online dating can enable older adults to connect with just the right partner.

What You're Looking For

At this point, you've done a lot of hard work to prepare yourself for the dating world. You've taken a realistic look at yourself and done a little sprucing up, and you've considered your bottom-line issues and values. Now it's time to consider what you are looking for in a mature dating partner.

TRAVELERS' TALES

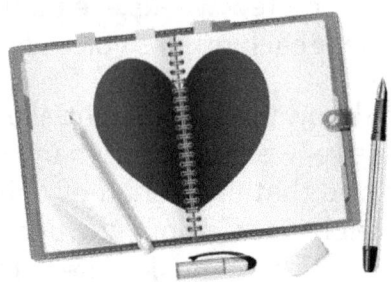

Participants in our Magic at Midlife survey described what they were looking for in a partner:

"Companionship, sexual attraction."

"Honest, non-deceptive, caring, loving, helpful, good listener, love me unconditionally."

"Intellectual compatibility, recreational compatibility, sexual compatibility."

"Mature, kind, active."

"Playfulness, curiosity, responsibility, warmth, intimacy, ability to care for oneself emotionally and speak up for one's needs, self-confidence, having a purpose in life, and that elusive 'spark.'"

"Honesty, honor, intelligence, humor, and bravery. Bravery to stand up for what he believes in, stay strong when scared, take the blame when it is his fault, change faults when needed. I would like to have these as my own characteristics as well! Still working on it."

"Work stability, sense of humor, someone to be my best friend and grow old with."

"Someone who would take in the love that I have,

someone who feels like home."

Many respondents mentioned intelligence, honesty, and humor as must-haves in a partner. With the exception of a desire for sexual attraction, survey participants didn't specify any particular physical characteristics. Nonetheless, you may have a physical "type" in mind. Remember your resolution to be a bit flexible in your search. Of course, you want to be with someone you find attractive, but a sense of physical attraction can grow when you are impressed by the essence of another human being. Don't immediately write potential partners off based on appearance, unless you're sure they are not for you.

Also remember that first dates can be awkward and just a little bit weird. Give people a chance beyond the first meeting if there's any spark at all. You can't possibly find out everything you want to know about someone in your first time together.

Too Young or Too Old to Be Your Partner?

As we said, when Jennifer and Charles met online, she was a little hesitant to pursue a relationship, because Charles, at 60, was seven years older than she. We're both glad that she didn't let a number stand in the way of true love, but we recognize that age can matter, and it may be a concern for you as you seek a partner.

In the United States today, most married couples consist of spouses who are within a year of each other's age, or a husband who is two to three years older than his wife. Despite all the jokes about "cougars," who are women involved with much younger men, most women select a mate who is the same age or older, sometimes considerably older. Because our society still supports the image of the older man and younger woman, there aren't huge numbers of women dating men several decades their junior. It is more likely that a man will have a younger partner in a male-female relationship.

This can become something of a problem as we age; since women tend to outlive men, the dating pool of older men shrinks over time. While the longevity gap between men and women is closing a bit (average life span for men is 76 years, while it is 83 years for women), it is still substantial.

Regardless of statistics, as you consider dating partners, you'll probably think about the age range that is comfortable for you. There are many factors to consider. We all know people who are roughly the same biological age who seem to be from different generations – the 60-year-old who is fit, vibrant, and engaged in life, as opposed to the 60-year-old who seems ready for the rocking chair on the front porch as a full-time pursuit. When we recently conducted a workshop on "Sex and Dating After 60," a couple of the gentleman participants said they were willing to date women their own age (about 70) but they couldn't find any 70-year-old women who were able to engage in the kind of vigorous activities they enjoy, such as hiking and mountain biking. A 50-year-old partner might be a better match for these youthful seniors!

If you're considering becoming involved with someone who is quite a bit older or younger, it's essential to be honest with yourself and each other about the challenges that may bring. What will a 15-year age difference look like 20 years from now? Is the issue of having children still on the table for either partner? Will differences in values and experiences be a problem? How will you handle aging (your own and your partner's)? Do you have similar goals and expectations? Are your sexual needs compatible? Will it be weird if your partner is close to the same age as your children (or your parents)?

Certainly couples with moderate or large age differences can have happy, healthy, fulfilling relationships. That's more likely to happen if you give the relationship time to mature before committing to each other, and keep your eyes open to what the age gap may mean in the long run.

Chapter 4: The Dating Game (It's Different Now)

> It started out slowly, it's coming on fast. I got a feeling it's gonna last. Timber, I'm falling in love.
> – Patty Loveless, "Timber, I'm Falling in Love"

The First Date

Some simple advice for the first date:

- ♥ Be safe – don't go anywhere isolated with a person you've only met online, for example.
- ♥ Do something interesting so you'll have something to talk about – you might see a movie, then have coffee.
- ♥ Consider a date that doesn't feel like a traditional date – a walk in the park, doing a volunteer activity together, or meeting for breakfast. This may feel less pressured.
- ♥ Remember the phrase "TMI" – too much information. You don't need to provide every detail of your divorce or your child's academic career on a first date.
- ♥ Listen. Ask intelligent questions. That's sexy.
- ♥ Stay sober. Enough said.
- ♥ Remember that if the date is a disaster, you'll have a juicy tale to tell!

Who Pays for What on a Date?

Many people who are new to the midlife dating scene are baffled about how to handle dating finances. Who should pick up the check?

Researchers conducted a survey of more than 17,000 single people, called "Who Pays for Dates?" Surprisingly, things haven't changed all that much over the past few decades. Both men and women mostly expect men to pay for dates, although men want women to offer to pay after they've been dating for a while. There are fascinating sociological implications of this study, but that doesn't really answer the question: *Should I pay the check?*

Money conversations with a person you hardly know (like a brand-new dating partner) can certainly be awkward. However, the question of who should pay can offer an excellent opportunity to start a relationship on the basis of honesty and open communication.

It really doesn't matter who pays for the first date. What matters is whether there is an overall sense of fairness and shared responsibility as the relationship progresses.

While one legitimate viewpoint is that men should pay most of the dating costs because there's still a wage gap between men and women, that doesn't address the specifics of a particular couple's situation.

There are two issues here: one is the actual cost of a date, and the other is who is hosting the date. Here are our specific suggestions for how to handle dating costs, based on our values about egalitarian relationships. See whether these ideas will work for you:

- ♥ Offer to split costs on the first date, but don't argue. If one person insists on paying, accept graciously.

- ♥ After the two of you have been dating a little while, have an honest conversation about wanting to share the costs. Be truthful about any financial limitations.

- ♥ For heaven's sake, don't get stuck in the stupid and sexist idea that a man who pays for a date is entitled to sexual favors. Many of the older women in the "Who Pays for Dates?" survey were worried about that, but it is mostly younger men who are dumb enough to think that way.

Paying for sex is sex trafficking, not dating.

- ♥ If one person makes a great deal more money than the other, the person who is not as well-to-do can still host a modest date. If Person A is the only one who can afford a fancy dinner and a show, Person B can reciprocate with a picnic and a free concert in the park. How much fun you have doesn't depend on how much you spend, but on each person taking the time and trouble to plan something you both will enjoy.

Falling in Love

Remember the incredible euphoria of falling in love? You can't think of anything else, you smile all the time, and the whole universe takes on a rosy glow. It doesn't matter whether you're 14 or 64, new love is an incomparable experience. Neuroscientists have found that the experience of falling in love activates the pleasure centers in the brain much like some drugs do, which is not surprising to anyone who has felt the intense joy of romantic love.

When you fall in love at 50 or 85, you may smile at yourself for feeling so much like a teenager. You do have the advantage of years of experience and wisdom, and (unlike a teen), you know that some of the glitter will wear off with time. Because of your experience, you also feel a profound gratitude that it's possible to have the champagne-bubble feeling of falling in love at your age. If you have done your homework as far as getting to know yourself, your values, and your goals in life, and you've picked your romantic partner accordingly, hang on and enjoy the ride.

We won't call this stage "infatuation," because that somehow implies it isn't real. It's very real, and can be one of the most enjoyable things in life. However, that ecstatic feeling, as you know, can't be the sole basis for making decisions for the future.

What we know, once we're in midlife or beyond, is that people can be deceptively charming in the first stages of a relationship. Even while your heart is throbbing away, your brain is evaluating the other person. If you've been hurt in a previous relationship after being sure that you had found "the one," you're even more likely to want to let time reveal whether that charmer is the real thing or not.

This is where a solid sense of yourself comes in handy. If you know you can not only survive but truly thrive on your own, you are less likely to overlook shortcomings in a potential partner. You can be honest with yourself about the positive and the negative qualities of your sweetie as they reveal themselves over time, and decide whether the whole picture is still what you want.

Sadly, no one is perfect. In the beginning of a thrilling relationship, however, we fall under the spell of attraction and believe that perfection is possible. As time goes on and you see each other more clearly, if you still like what you see, the relationship can evolve into a mature, lasting love. That's pretty thrilling, too, especially at our age.

Timing Is Everything

Having a realistic understanding of the first exciting phase of a relationship and the more subdued phases that follow is important in evaluating whether things are going well between you. Here are some questions to ask yourself:

- ♥ Does your potential partner "overshare" early in the relationship, such as discussing everything that went wrong in previous relationships on your first couple of dates?
- ♥ Does your sweetheart continue to make an effort to please you, even after the initial phase of your relationship?
- ♥ Does your dating partner expect you to commit before you have really had a chance to get to know each other?
- ♥ Is your sweetheart willing to let you move forward in the

relationship at your own pace?
- ♥ Does your possible mate use good judgment about when to introduce you to their children (especially if they are minors) and when to meet yours?
- ♥ Do you both make the relationship a priority as time goes on?
- ♥ Can you talk openly together about how things are going between the two of you?
- ♥ Do you both use good judgment about gift-giving (in other words, no expensive gifts early on)?
- ♥ Is it important to each of you to continue getting to know the other person throughout the relationship, rather than assuming you already know everything?
- ♥ Have the two of you become a "we" at the appropriate time?
- ♥ Do you feel as though you each have a similar investment in the relationship, or is one person more invested?

Older Hearts Break, Too

When you choose to enter the dating arena, you are taking risks – the risk of being rejected; the risk of thinking you have found someone wonderful, only to be disillusioned; the risk of breaking up; and the risk of a broken heart. These risks are unavoidable. We hope they don't happen to you, but they might.

Rejection is painful, whether you are 16 or 60. It can happen in the initial stages, when people are often judged on superficial characteristics such as physical attractiveness or wealth. It may hurt even more if you have taken the time to get to know someone, only to be told that they aren't interested in you.

If you read this book carefully, you are less likely to be surprised and disillusioned by a potential partner, because you'll know what to look out for. However, some people are really, really good at disguising their true nature, and even the smartest and most savvy folks can be duped.

Breaking up can happen because you simply aren't compatible with each other, or because the timing is wrong for one of you. For example, you may have been single for a long time and are now ready for a committed relationship, only to find yourself attracted to a newly divorced person who just wants to play the field at this point. Bummer.

Rejection is so painful because we usually take it as a sign that there is something wrong with us. That hurts. If you can look beyond the hurt to see if there is anything you can learn that will help you to have a healthier relationship in the future, great. If not, this is the time for support and comfort from your friends and family, and for kindness from yourself. Platitudes such as "Maybe it just wasn't meant to be" or "There are plenty of other fish in the sea" may not help much, but that doesn't mean they aren't true. Maybe it wasn't meant to be, and the obnoxious tactics your partner used during the breakup were an indication that you would have been miserable in a long-term relationship with this person. There are, in fact, enough other fish in the sea that you can most likely find a compatible mate in time, so don't give up hope.

After a breakup, you are in great jeopardy of dwelling on your resentment and bitterness. Some of this is normal and human, and hopefully you have a good friend or two who is willing to let you talk it all out. However, if it gets to the point that your friends are avoiding you because they're tired of hearing you say rotten things about your ex, it's time to move on emotionally. One more platitude that is true: Living well really IS the best revenge.

Speaking of jeopardy, be aware that leaving an abusive partner places you at risk. Quite a bit of physical and sexual violence occurs at or after the time of a separation. If you are fearful about telling your partner you want to end the relationship (for any reason), seek help in advance. Talk to an advocate at a domestic violence agency about your worries and develop a safety plan (remember, these are free, confidential services). Even if there has not been overt violence in the relationship, trust your gut if you are afraid to leave. If your partner has been controlling, jealous, threatening, or verbally demeaning, those are warning signs that the breakup may become dangerous.

If abuse is not an issue, you still may come to the point where you know that this relationship is simply not for you, and you may have to initiate a breakup. This can be painful as well. Most of us don't like to hurt other people. Older folks often have the additional burden of feeling as though they have failed when a relationship falls apart. For example, individuals ending a second or third (or subsequent) marriage can feel as though there must be something wrong with them.

When you know a relationship is over, it is unkind to be evasive about your feelings. Talk to a trusted friend or a therapist if you're worried about how to explain the need to move on. Give your partner the respect of having an open, honest conversation describing your feelings and the reasons for them. Be prepared for anger and blame from your partner, and vow not to react in kind. Allow your partner the opportunity to ask questions, to express a range of feelings, and to have time to process what you are saying. Take the high road by sharing responsibility for the failure of the relationship and by making your explanation as kind as possible under the circumstances.

Hold your head high after a rejection or a breakup. You are still the same attractive, funny, smart, kind person you were the day before, and it's the other person's loss if they don't recognize you for the gem you are. Your goal is to find someone who thinks you are incredibly wonderful and special. You don't want to be with anyone who thinks any less of you.

By the way, if you're wondering whether your partner is losing interest in you, sadly, the answer is probably yes – at least if the behavior goes on for an extended period of time. If your sweetheart is always too busy, too tired, or too unavailable to be with you, take the hint. The books *He's Just Not That Into You* and *She's Just Not That Into You* were bestsellers because they told it like it is: a person who cares about you makes it pretty obvious. If you find yourself making up excuses for an indifferent or not-very-kind partner, stop. Make your expectations clear, ask for what you want, and if it's not forthcoming, realize that the relationship is not viable.

Ultimately, you have to decide whether you want to be with your partner or not. Remember that while you may want a relationship very badly, you can be okay by yourself. A bad relationship is much, much worse than no relationship. A fundamentally good relationship may go through rough times, especially when one or both partners are under significant stress, but you probably know in your heart whether the relationship is healthy and supports your best self. If you're indecisive about what to do, you may want to talk to a counselor or therapist to clarify your priorities and choose a path.

TRAVELERS' TALES

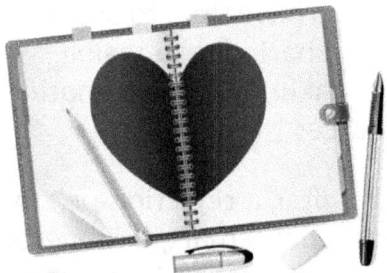

DeShawn is in his fifties and has been seeing Wanda for several months now. At first, he thought she was great. She seemed warm and kind, and was very interested in him. However, as time went on, DeShawn recognized that Wanda was very emotionally needy and couldn't function independently.

She lived with her sister and hadn't held any job for more than a year. She had no friends and few interests of her own. Wanda couldn't seem to entertain herself when DeShawn was busy with his regular job or his freelance web design business. She called him more than 15 times a day, even though he asked her to limit calls while he was working. Also, she seemed really upset if a day went by when they couldn't be together, even at the very beginning of their relationship.

DeShawn tried to make time for Wanda, and cut back his freelance work on the weekends. Eventually, however, he realized that he was more annoyed than intrigued by their relationship. He tried to talk to her tactfully about the possibility of going their separate ways, but Wanda became hysterical, crying and wailing, and said that if he broke up with her, she didn't think she could go on. She had told DeShawn that she had attempted suicide twice before when previous relationships had ended.

DeShawn felt tied up in knots. It became increasingly clear to him that he didn't want to continue his relationship with Wanda, but he didn't want to be responsible for her suicide, either. He suggested that she see a therapist, but she refused. She began calling him at all hours of the night and showing up at his house unannounced. DeShawn tried ignoring her calls, but she left dozens of messages on his phone, some saying she felt like killing herself and that it would be all his fault.

Finally, DeShawn had had enough. A friend told him about the National Suicide Hotline, and he called to get advice about how to handle the situation with Wanda. He talked to Wanda's sister so she would know what was going on.

DeShawn invited Wanda to a coffee shop to talk in a public place. There he told her that he cared about her, but that he realized their relationship just wasn't meant to be. He gave her the phone number for the National Suicide Hotline, saying that he hoped she would keep herself safe and reach out for help if she needed it, but that he couldn't stay with her for that reason alone. DeShawn added that he was sure she wouldn't want him to maintain the relationship just because he was worried about her. He said that he wouldn't be taking any calls from her, and that he expected her to respect his wishes by not showing up at his house.

DeShawn was prepared to get an anti-harassment order through the court if her behavior continued, but he did not tell her this. Also, following the advice from the National Suicide Hotline, he worked hard to keep his tone of voice calm and to not react when Wanda got worked up. He had previously arranged for her sister to come pick Wanda up at the coffee shop, which she did.

Afterward DeShawn felt relieved, but still a bit worried. He reached out to some of his friends, who reassured him that he had done all he could, and that Wanda's actions in the future were her responsibility.

SECTION THREE: AM I ON THE RIGHT ROAD?

SECTION THREE: AM I ON THE RIGHT ROAD?

Chapter 5: Can I Trust This Person?

> I never knew a man could tell so many lies,
> he had a different story for every set of eyes.
> How can he remember who he's talking to?
> – Neil Young, "Ambulance Blues"

Sizing Up a Potential Partner

Have you ever had a friend who began a relationship that had disaster written all over it from the beginning? Right away, it's clear to you that Mr. or Ms. Wrong is a catastrophe waiting to happen. You know, for example, that your friend is unlikely to have a satisfying long-term relationship with someone who drinks too much, flies off the handle at the slightest provocation, is overly involved in someone else's life, or never seems to shoulder any responsibilities whatsoever. Your friend seems to be thinking only with their heart, not their head.

If you're looking for your own potential sweetheart, you want both your heart and your head involved in the assessment. That's usually easier to do if you identify your requirements ahead of time and try to take an objective look at a dating partner before you get too involved.

Here are a few things to ask yourself as you choose the must-haves that make sense to you.

- ♥ Does Potential Sweetheart tell the truth?
- ♥ Does Potential Sweetheart have a steady job or a regular activity (such as volunteer work) that reflects some effort and meaning?
- ♥ Can Potential Sweetheart take care of basic daily needs (like meals and laundry) independently, if physically able to do so?
- ♥ Does Potential Sweetheart meet financial obligations?

- ♥ Can Potential Sweetheart manage the stresses of everyday life without turning to alcohol, drugs, gambling, or other self-destructive behaviors?
- ♥ Does Potential Sweetheart manage emotions successfully most of the time?
- ♥ Can Potential Sweetheart deal with anger without shouting, cursing, blaming, hitting, or pouting?
- ♥ Is Potential Sweetheart appropriately independent of family (or does 90-year-old Mama have to make a wake-up call every morning?)
- ♥ If Potential Sweetheart is a parent, are parenting responsibilities handled with love, appropriate boundaries, and realistic expectations?
- ♥ Does Potential Sweetheart take care of health matters and value wellness?
- ♥ Has Potential Sweetheart set long-term goals and achieved them, even though it was difficult?
- ♥ Will Potential Sweetheart do necessary chores and duties without being nagged?
- ♥ Can Potential Sweetheart set aside their own needs when someone else's needs legitimately should take priority?
- ♥ Is Potential Sweetheart fair in dealings with you and others?
- ♥ Can Potential Sweetheart speak up and identify what they need from you?
- ♥ Does Potential Sweetheart treat others with respect and consideration, even when there's nothing tangible to be gained?
- ♥ Does Potential Sweetheart think you are very special, and treat you that way over the course of time?

If you look back at failed relationships, you'll probably find that your partner didn't meet some of these important criteria. Many of these items are the basis of responsible adult behavior, and if you are looking for a partner, it never hurts to seek a responsible adult. If a "bad boy" or "bad girl" appeals to you, ask yourself honestly if you're trying to be a rescuer or deluding yourself that you can make another individual change.

You'll find more details about these concerns throughout Section Three. If Potential Sweetheart matches your selection from the above requirements (and feel free to add your own), you have a decent chance of creating a fulfilling relationship with each other. Have fun!

Run, Don't Walk, to the Nearest Exit!

The last thing you want in a midlife relationship is a partner who makes you miserable, takes advantage of you, or hurts you emotionally or physically. There are no guarantees that you can avoid bad experiences, but learning the red flags can help (see also the Chapter 2 discussion, "Identify and Deal with Past Abuse").

People are typically quite charming at the beginning of a relationship – including those who turn out to be unkind or even dangerous. In fact, abusive people are often initially particularly charming. They may make it their business to lure potential partners into a relationship, only to exploit or harm them after trust has been established.

Even if you are 50 or 60 or older, let's face it, you may be somewhat naïve when it comes to dating relationships. When Jennifer, age 53 and widowed, met Charles, the majority of her dating experience had been during her teenage years. She had all the sophistication of a 15-year-old when it came to a new romance. In fact, that's one of the reasons we wrote this book. We want to educate older folks about the pleasures and pitfalls of finding a suitable and wonderful partner.

Remember how you took a look at your past relationships and identified hints that they were headed in the wrong direction?

There are some warning signs you can learn to look out for in any relationship:

- Moving too fast – someone who tells you "I love you" on the second date
- Moving too slow – someone who doesn't say "I love you" long after you have committed to the relationship
- Controlling behavior – treating you like a child, telling you what to wear, disregarding your preferences, violating your privacy
- Excessive jealousy – this is not a sign of true love; it's a sign of insecurity and possible danger
- Lack of respect – if you don't feel respected, this is a HUGE red flag
- Lack of reciprocity – taking without giving back, creating imbalances in the relationship
- Alcohol or drug abuse – you can't fix this in someone else, and it will only get worse; if you are unsure whether the behaviors you are seeing point to substance abuse, find out
- Physical violence of any sort – don't make excuses; this is a line that can't be crossed
- Sexual coercion – if you don't feel you can say "no" without making your partner angry, this is a very bad sign
- Financial irresponsibility – not taking care of financial obligations, not caring about being in debt, gambling, spending money beyond their means
- Poor interactions with everyone else – if the person has only negative relationships in his or her life, perhaps this is not everyone else's fault

Trust your instincts. If you believe the person you are seeing is moving too fast in the relationship, slow it down. If they won't take the hint, that's trouble. Remember that extreme jealousy is not a sign of love; it's an indication that the person wants to control you.

Here are the biggest "green flags" that let you know your sweetie is a good guy or gal:

- ♥ The 3 Cs – compassion, consideration, clear communication (see Chapter 6)
- ♥ Respect for your opinions and boundaries
- ♥ Fairness
- ♥ Reasonable control of moods
- ♥ Acting appropriately for the stage of the relationship

It's sad but true that there are people out there who are interested in financially or sexually exploiting others, or who want someone to control and abuse. Use your head as well as your heart in your relationship choices. If something does go wrong and you don't feel safe, don't hesitate to call for advice. As mentioned previously, domestic violence and sexual assault advocacy agencies offer free, confidential help for people of all ages. National hotlines that can provide information and guide you to local agencies are listed in the Resources section at the end of this book.

Set Your Trust Meter

Bad experiences earlier in life can make you either too trusting, or not trusting enough. It's as though we have a "trust meter" that should be calibrated to reality, but instead is set and reset by our relationships and expectations.

Trust has a natural timeline. You may get a good feeling about a person right away (in fact, you may be head-over-heels in love before you know it), but keep your wits about you and let yourself learn the person's true character over time.

If you have a consistent pattern of being hurt by others, you may be too trusting. When you look back, you tell yourself that you should have seen the signs that the person was not trustworthy, but at the time, you wanted to believe the best. People who are too trusting tend to trust everyone but themselves – they ignore their instincts and the "gut feeling" that tells them to beware.

If you know you have a habit of trusting in situations when, in hindsight, you wish you had not, set some limits for yourself. For example, you may decide not to lend or give money to a relationship partner. If you have unthinkingly trusted an addict or alcoholic, give Al-Anon a chance, and read about codependency (see Melody Beattie's classic book *Codependent No More*). Most of all, give yourself time to learn whether a potential partner is trustworthy. Consistent positive behavior in a variety of situations over a long period of time (years, not weeks) is the best indicator of trustworthiness.

If your family and friends seem alarmed by your partner for some reason, pay attention. They could be wrong, of course, but there could be some reasonable basis for their concern. Try not to be defensive, and ask them for specific examples of your partner's behaviors that have generated their anxiety. Then pay attention to these behaviors and see what you think.

Trusting too little is the other side of the coin. When you have been hurt by someone (or a string of someones), your trust meter may be reset so low that only Superman or Superwoman could earn your trust. The danger here is that you may create the very situation that you fear. Nothing damages a relationship like suspiciousness and jealousy.

TRAVELERS' TALES

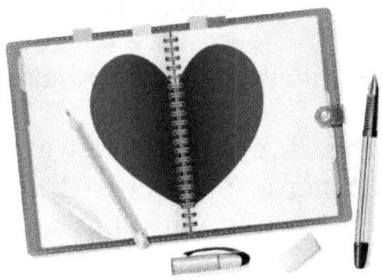

Vilmar is a 63-year-old man who was in a long-term relationship that ended when he discovered his partner was cheating. He then met Ari, who is slightly younger and seems to be as kind as he is charming. Ari lost his last partner to death, and told Vilmar that he had been faithful throughout the relationship and valued monogamy highly. While Ari has not given Vilmar any particular reason to be jealous, he is a friendly person and willing to talk to just about anyone. Vilmar is still reeling from his past partner's deception, and he begins to question Ari about every encounter, to check up on his whereabouts, and to worry if Ari is even a little bit late. Instead of making Vilmar feel more secure, this behavior is pushing Ari away, and Vilmar is afraid that Ari will end the relationship. The more Vilmar fears losing Ari, the more he acts in a way that creates distance.

Excessive jealousy is a relationship killer. While it's human to be a bit jealous at times, if you can't trust your partner, something is truly wrong. Either you are with the wrong person (because you have picked up on signals that your sweetheart is not to be trusted) or you're hypersensitive to this issue because of your own experiences. It's sometimes hard to sort this out. A therapist or a trusted friend can help, and you may just have to decide to proceed slowly in the relationship until you get the true picture.

Meanwhile, take responsibility for your own actions and "fake it till you make it" by acting as though you are not crazed with jealousy. Work on building the positive aspects of the relationship and your own self-confidence, and see what develops.

The bottom line is this: If your partner isn't trustworthy, what the heck are you doing together? If your partner is trustworthy, why are you driving him or her nuts with your suspicions?

Should You Do a Background Check?

Hmm. This is a tough one. The answer depends on where your trust meter is set, how you got to know your potential partner, and what other sources of information you may have.

When Jennifer and Charles met online through a dating website, she couldn't control her curiosity and she googled him. The first result indicated that he was 81 years old, but then she realized that this was his father, who had the same name! A couple of months after we met (and, to tell the truth, we both fell in love fairly quickly), Jennifer got a phone call from a friend who worked for another branch of the government agency where Charles was working. Her friend (we'll call her Linda) told Jennifer, excitedly, "He's all right!" "What?" "That guy you told me you met online – Charles Peck. He's all right!" It turned out that Linda had gone to a national convention and met someone who worked with Charles. She asked the woman what she knew about him, and was told, "He is a real gentleman. He's one of my favorite people. I've known him for years, and he is always willing to help people out. He is a man of his word."

In fact, Linda was the only one of Jennifer's friends who asked what Charles's last name was, a fact Jennifer found a bit curious. Later, she understood that Linda was looking out for her and intended to find out what she could about this mysterious "Charles Peck."

If you fall in love with someone you've known since high school, you probably have all the information you need about their trustworthiness. However, if you meet someone online or in a bar, take your time and use common sense, of course. At a minimum, most people will look at publicly available information such as a Facebook page or Twitter account, and conduct a basic web search. If you have minor children or grandchildren in your home (ever), it is wise to do a sex offender search, but be aware that only a tiny fraction of sex offenders are ever caught and convicted.

If you choose to do a background check, do it very early in the relationship. Most people can understand reasonable caution about strangers, but may feel betrayed if you check up on them after you've been dating for some time. For information on how to do a free online background check, see this article from *USA Today*: http://usat.ly/Z3zXf5 If this link is no longer available, search for similar information from a reputable source (not someone trying to sell you background checks).

Privacy, Boundaries, and Trust

According to a 2010 survey by Retrevo.com (a consumer electronics shopping and review site), 29 percent of people in dating couples have checked the email or call history of their partner without permission – in other words, they snooped. Younger people were more likely to snoop – older people grew up with a greater expectation of privacy.

Before you conclude that your partner has violated your trust, be sure that you have had clear communication about boundaries and behavior. For example, you might assume that because you've been dating for a couple of months, your partner should be seeing only you, while the other person might consider dating several people at once to be perfectly fine, unless there is an explicit agreement to be monogamous.

Also, think about what is okay to you and what is not, and have that conversation. Do you feel comfortable with your partner being close friends with a former intimate? What kind of social interaction makes you uncomfortable? For example, if you are in a heterosexual relationship, are you comfortable with your partner having dinner alone with an acquaintance of the opposite sex? Is it okay with you if your partner goes out drinking and dancing without you? Again, don't make assumptions. Talk about what each of you finds acceptable, and why.

Some common areas of conflict are email or chat relationships that your partner insists are only platonic but is secretive about, or the use of pornography. If you are both fine with private interactions even once the relationship has progressed to the committed stage, no problem. If not, this is something to discuss. If you have differing views about the use of pornography, again, this is a conversation you need to have. You should never be forced to view pornography or use it as part of your sex life if it is distasteful to you, but you're unlikely to be able to change your partner's pornography viewing habits at this stage of life. You may have to agree to disagree and set up conditions (such as private use) that you can live with.

Chapter 6: Is Your Sweetheart a Grown-up?

> If you're immature, I'm out the door.
> – Lil Kim, "Dreams"

How Do You Measure Maturity?

You are certainly well aware that the number of birthdays a person has celebrated does not equal a maturity score! A person in their eighties can be childish and immature, while someone decades younger can be mature and responsible.

Immature people can be charming and fun to be around, but they don't work very well as partners in committed relationships. What usually happens is that you find yourself exasperated by the very same carefree characteristics that attracted you in the first place. On the other hand, people who have lost all of their childlike qualities can be boring and controlling.

Way back in the 1960s, Eric Berne, MD, wrote a book called *Games People Play* (1964), explaining how people relate to each other. He said we each have three components of our personality (similar to Freud's superego, ego, and id) that determine our relationships. The description below is our own oversimplified but useful version of Berne's concepts, describing the parts of our personality and how they direct our actions:

> **Parent** – this is the part of our personality that directs, scolds, and nurtures others. In **Controlling Parent mode,** we tell people what to do, criticize them, and judge them. In **Nurturing Parent mode,** we support, guide, lead, protect, and comfort others.
>
> **Adult** – this is the part of our personality that can navigate relationships with maturity. In **Adult**

mode, we can negotiate, compromise, express our needs appropriately, and take other people's needs into account. We behave assertively and reasonably in Adult mode.

Child – this is the part of our personality that can be both delightful and infuriating. In **Irresponsible or Rebellious Child mode,** we drink too much, gamble, avoid obligations, refuse reasonable requests, and generally act carefree when we should not. In **Playful Child mode,** we can have fun, be creative, laugh, and bring a sense of delight and playfulness to our interactions.

Each of us has the capacity to act in all three of these modes, but we tend to have a preferred pattern. What's interesting is the way in which we react to others. For example, if your partner is acting bossy and superior (Controlling Parent mode), you may very well revert to Rebellious Child mode: "Don't tell me what to do!" Then the two of you will probably go several rounds stuck in these roles before (hopefully) one of you goes into Adult mode and tries to work out a reasonable solution.

Couples can get stuck in the Parent-Child dynamic for a very long time. If you are looking for a rescuer because you don't feel you can manage your own life, you will likely find someone who is most comfortable in Parent mode. Perhaps the two of you will play these roles out permanently, but if you get your own act together and want to have a more egalitarian relationship, your Parent-type partner may not be flexible enough to change, and the relationship may break down. If you have spent most of your life caring for others and are attracted by the charm of a Child-type partner, you may grow weary of being the only functional adult in the relationship.

Jennifer found that explaining these roles to the couples she treated in therapy was extremely helpful. Once they recognized what they were doing, clients could begin to talk about how things were playing out, and to make other choices. It is human nature to blame the other person and believe that if only he or she would change, the relationship would be perfect. In fact, we become involved in elaborate relationship "dances" in which one partner's behavior triggers a predictable pattern of behavior by the other. The bad news is that the only person you can change is yourself; the good news is that by changing your own behavior, you can initiate a change in the relationship. If the bond between the two of you is strong and your partner is basically a decent person, there is a good chance that your individual changes can create the momentum for a positive shift in the relationship.

Work and Financial Stability

Just as women complain that most men are only looking for physical attractiveness, many men complain that women (and some men) are searching for a sugar daddy who can offer them financial benefits. Surely we should be beyond these sex role stereotypes, and it's time to simply look at how a potential partner handles their financial obligations.

Danger signs include:

- Not being able to keep a job
- Having a huge amount of debt without good reason (such as a medical catastrophe)
- Chronic complaints about bosses, co-workers, and work environments, even after changing jobs multiple times
- A pattern of having been fired from jobs
- Big stacks of unpaid bills
- Spending sprees that don't seem to make financial sense
- Gambling that leads to financial hardships
- Lying about money
- Borrowing money without repaying it

- Being unable to meet basic living expenses, unless there are extenuating circumstances
- Unfairness in sharing expenses
- Your feeling exploited or resentful about financial arrangements

While you may overlook some wonderful people if you are a snob about status and wealth, it's reasonable to look for someone who has a job (or had one) that reflects some effort and meaning. Volunteer work counts as well, as does creative effort. The financially unsuccessful artist who works at a menial job is worthy of respect, but you have to be honest about whether you will be resentful if you connect with someone who is struggling to pay the bills.

For more about money matters once you are in a relationship, see Chapter 14. At this point, your task is to think about your own money values and what you expect from a partner, and to observe whether a potential partner is handling financial responsibilities appropriately.

Emotional Regulation and Stress Management

Jennifer once attended a training on Couples Therapy in which the presenter, Richard Stuart, remarked, "No one ever farts on a first date." This was actually a profound piece of wisdom. We all put on our best face when we first meet someone. We would never fuss at someone for a trivial behavior on a first date, for example. If we are crabby or upset, we probably do our best to hide it.

As relationships progress, however, it's normal and natural to express a wider range of emotion. Since no one is perfect, we will all raise our voices, say something unkind, cry, act grumpy, or be critical at some point in a relationship. Most of us have the capacity to recognize when we are being unreasonable, to apologize, and to do our best to control our behavior as time goes on – at least until the next very bad day.

Some people, though, either don't make the effort or are unable to control their emotions to a reasonable extent. Once the "honeymoon phase" of the relationship is over, they display irritability, anger, or sadness inappropriately and frequently. Certain people have mental health problems or personality disorders that make emotional regulation difficult or nearly impossible; others have addictions that fuel their emotional unpredictability. Some people are so self-absorbed or hostile that they are not concerned about the effects of their behavior on a partner, or they use emotional expression (such as anger) to try to control the other person.

When you love someone and they develop a mental health problem or addiction, you may very well decide to hang in there, help them, and try to get through it together. This is a tough decision in a long-term relationship and it takes a lot of soul-searching to figure out what to do. At the initial stage of a relationship, however, you probably don't want to step into that quagmire.

While only you can decide what you are willing to deal with, think long and hard before settling into a relationship with someone who has adult temper tantrums; who uses alcohol, drugs, food, self-injury, or gambling to self-soothe; who takes out frustrations by directing anger at you, a child, a pet, or anyone vulnerable; who behaves in ways you consider unacceptable, such as cursing, blaming, hitting, or extended pouting; who scares you; or who makes you miserable on a regular basis.

Self-Reliance

TRAVELERS' TALES

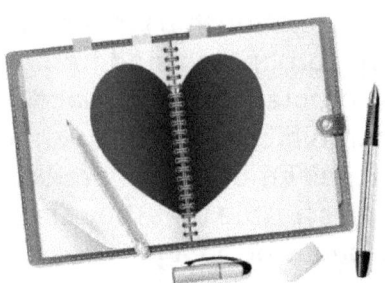

Indy was in her late forties when she met Georgianna, who was about the same age. Georgianna seemed pleasant and the two of them got along well. One day, Georgianna was talking about how hard it was to wake up in the morning, and she mentioned that her mother called her every day at 6:00 a.m. to make sure she got up in time for work. At first, Indy thought she was joking, but she soon learned that Georgianna relied on her mother for financial assistance as well as daily reminders. Georgianna and her mother talked on the phone several times each day, and Georgianna brought her laundry over for her mother to wash and dry. Georgianna revealed that a couple of previous relationships had broken up because her partners didn't want to compete with her mother for Georgianna's time. Indy began wondering whether Georgianna was able to function as an independent adult.

By the time a person hits 40, he or she should be able to take care of basic daily needs independently, barring disability. Sometimes people emerging from long-term relationships expect their new partner to take on the tasks that their ex formerly did for them, such as cooking, doing laundry, or mowing the lawn. While it is okay to work out sharing the tasks of living, each person should be able to manage alone if necessary. At the beginning of a relationship, especially, it is a little weird if you find your partner expects you to wash their dirty clothes, for example.

Look around your new sweetheart's home. It doesn't have to be a showplace, but if there are dishes piled high in the sink, laundry that smells like a bad day in the gym, unpaid bills stacked up, and a neglected yard, think about what it would be like to function as a team in a household. Of course, if the person is ill or has a disability that makes it difficult to complete chores, that is one thing. If he or she is just plain lazy or feels entitled to have someone else do the picking up, you may want to reconsider a serious relationship.

Another part of self-reliance is taking reasonable care of one's health. A person with diabetes who binges on sweets or a woman who has avoided mammograms for the past 20 years is not handling responsibility well.

Be careful about getting into the role of rescuer with someone who is not self-reliant. If your partner can't function independently, and you rush in to help, you are setting up a dynamic that may be very uncomfortable in the long run. This doesn't mean you should avoid helping out or being supportive, of course, but do keep a sense of perspective about the other person's life skills.

Relationships with Others

It can be very tempting to be the one person your partner admires and treats well, but if his or her other relationships are a disaster, tread with care. Remember that you are still in the honeymoon stage at the beginning of a relationship. Does your partner speak of an ex with disdain and hostility? What about your partner's relationship with children, if there are any? Is this person respected and admired by others – friends, family, co-workers, and neighbors?

This is a very good reason to let the courtship phase extend a while longer. You can do a better job evaluating your partner's other relationships and general "people skills" if you have the opportunity to be together in a variety of situations and observe how your partner gets along with people in different roles.

Sense of Purpose and Achievement

What kinds of things would a person need to do to gain your respect? Consider whether your partner meets those criteria. Here is where your values come into play. For us, there were certain qualities that we each prized and looked for. Jennifer was impressed that Charles had gone back to college and graduated with a bachelor's degree in his early fifties. She also liked the way he talked about the challenges he had faced in his work life. For example, while working as a carpenter in a facility for residents with developmental disabilities, he prided himself on creating innovative adaptive equipment that would meet an individual resident's needs. He also demonstrated compassion and respect for those residents. Charles was impressed with Jennifer's academic accomplishments and her dedication to her work with survivors of abuse. Both of us valued lifelong learning and enjoyed writing (hence this book!).

The 3 Cs: How to Know You've Found a Winner

If you are wondering whether your dating partner is truly a good person, pay close attention to the 3 Cs – compassion, consideration, and communication.

Compassion

A person with true compassion is able to empathize and has a sense of perspective about what is important in life. Compassionate people don't say cruel things, even in a joking manner. They are able to see the range of human motivation and accountability. They can understand that a good person can do something wrong, and that someone can have more than one reason for a particular behavior. In other words, they don't see the world or other people as black-and-white extremes.

Consideration

If we had to pick one characteristic in a partner for any of our children, it would most likely be consideration. A considerate person cares deeply about their partner's well-being, comfort, health, and happiness. The most pain in relationships usually comes from narcissistic, or self-absorbed, partners. Their own happiness is front and center, and they will trample their partners to attain self-satisfaction. Look for small signs of ongoing consideration, such as a partner who always considers your needs in making decisions. Don't confuse consideration with a lack of self-respect; you don't want a partner who can't identify or communicate their legitimate needs. But a considerate partner will help you feel loved, respected, and cherished.

Clear Communication

We can't emphasize this characteristic too much. A partner with good communication skills can be your co-creator of a healthy and fulfilling relationship. A partner with poor communication skills (one who is unwilling or unable to talk things out with you) will make it very difficult to work together to meet both of your needs.

Chapter 7: Will Our Lives Fit Together?

> Thinking is the best way to travel.
> – The Moody Blues, "The Best Way to Travel"

Starting a New Relationship Before Your Kids Are Grown

People are having children later in life, so if you're considering a new romantic relationship after age 40, you or your potential partner may still have young children or teenagers at home. Most parents worry about bringing a new person into their kids' lives. It can be complicated to balance your desire for a fabulous new relationship with your responsibilities and love for your children. Here are a few things to consider:

- ♥ If the person you are interested in has minor children who live with the other parent, don't assume that they will always live elsewhere and just visit you. That situation can always change.

- ♥ Pay attention to how potential partners handle problems and issues with their kids or yours. Is their style loving, distant, or overly involved?

- ♥ If your sweetie has young kids or teens, what are their needs and are you prepared to help meet them? When Jennifer was dating, she met a nice man who had custody of a teenage daughter who had major problems (including self-injury). Had the relationship progressed, this would have been a big consideration.

- ♥ Don't fool yourself that your potential partner's kids' issues won't affect you, because they certainly will if you enter a long-term relationship.

- ♥ Someone who doesn't have a loving relationship with theirown children is unlikely to have one with your kids.

Because of her many years of experience working with sexual abuse and assault survivors, Jennifer particularly wants to highlight the need for caution when bringing another adult into a home with children. Child abusers are often superficially charming, and they engage in a process called "grooming" with both potential child victims and the adults responsible for those children. When an abuser grooms a child, he makes the child feel special and works on establishing a close, secretive relationship. (We say "he" because the vast majority of sexual abusers are male, but women can be sexually abusive as well.) Some pedophiles (people who are sexually attracted to children) make a special effort to date single women with kids in order to victimize the children. Teens can be the target of predators as well.

We don't mention this to scare you or to discourage you from developing a relationship while your kids are growing up, but greater knowledge can lead to improved safety for your family. For example, don't assume that because a potential partner has a clean background check, he is not a sex offender – only a very small percentage of abusers are caught and convicted.

You can increase your knowledge about how to protect your kids from abuse. Some communities offer programs such as *Darkness to Light* (www.d2l.org) to educate parents. Gavin De Becker's book *Protecting the Gift: Keeping Children and Teenagers Safe (and Parents Sane)* offers a great deal of information about spotting predators. Boys Town Press publishes a book called *Unmasking Sexual Con Games* in versions for both parents and teens. Your local sexual assault advocacy program will also most likely offer community education programs and a confidential person to talk to if you have concerns.

Children can be physically and emotionally, as well as sexually, abused by their parents' partners. Establishing a solid relationship and open communication with your children is a great start in protecting them, and simply listening and observing interactions with your child and your partner can tell you a lot. All this cautionary information needs to be taken in context. Many children have highly beneficial relationships with stepparents or parents' partners. Nonetheless, in the search stage of your journey, your first priority will be to do your best to ensure your children's safety when choosing a partner. See Chapter 15 for more information about blending families.

Consider Responsibilities for Aging Parents

Even if you or your potential partner is well up in years, one or both of you may have aging parents to consider. We discuss including parents in your life together in Chapter 15. In the early stages of a relationship, however, as you evaluate whether your lives will fit together, there are some important questions you will want to consider:

- ♥ What is your partner's relationship with their parents?
- ♥ What are the current caretaking responsibilities?
- ♥ What is the expectation of future responsibilities?
- ♥ Do you or your partner expect parents to live with you?
- ♥ If so, who is expected to do the lion's share of caretaking?
- ♥ Are you in agreement about how you would care for an ill or dependent parent or other relative?

Fitting In with Friends

When you meet your partner in midlife, you probably have friends who are important to you. It's always interesting to see how your friends react to your new love interest, what they think, and how everyone gets along.

If you've been single for a while and you have a best friend or a close circle of friends, there may be an adjustment period as you incorporate your sweetheart into your life. In truth, there may be a little jealousy or jockeying for position, because your attention is absorbed by your new relationship.

As things settle down, it can be a challenge to balance your time and attention between your friends and your partner, particularly if one of you is more social than the other. In some cases, you may enjoy time with your sweetheart and friends, old or new. In other situations, it may work best if you and your old buddy spend time alone together, doing your usual things.

As we age, friendships become even more vital. Studies have shown that people with positive social connections stay healthier and more intellectually sharp. When the inevitable challenges of our older years come to pass, such as an ailing spouse, the support of friends can make all the difference. So don't let your friendships fade in the light of your love relationship.

People vary greatly in how much social contact they enjoy or crave. Even a dedicated introvert can benefit from time with others. It may be easier for someone who is not naturally comfortable in social settings to make connections in a structured environment, such as a class or a volunteer project. If your partner would rather stay home and do crossword puzzles while you socialize, don't push. Everyone has the right to choose their own level of interaction. Talk to each other and plan social activities that work for both of you. Scale down the size of your parties, if crowds make your sweetheart break out in a sweat. Offer to go to the most important events for your partner, such as the office holiday party, while declining other invitations that you don't think you'll enjoy.

What if you really don't like your partner's buddies? Think about the reasons. Do you feel jealous, because their relationship goes "way back"? Are you bothered by their activities, such as going out drinking or taking a three-week motorcycle trip without you? Is it just a matter of incompatible personalities? Depending on the issue, try to find a work-around. If you find their friend loud and obnoxious, visit briefly and then find somewhere else to be. If you don't like what they do together, this is really a concern about your partner and your relationship, not the friends.

If your friends dislike your partner, try to consider what is going on without getting defensive. Love truly is blind–if several friends don't like your sweetie, they may be seeing something you aren't, and this may warrant a second look. Perhaps what you see as protectiveness, they see as coercion and control – and it is just possible they are right.

What if your partner has a friend of the opposite sex (or, if you are gay or lesbian, of the same sex)? You have to be honest with yourself and your sweetheart about what makes you uncomfortable and why. If they are truly just "buddies" and have been in a brotherly or sisterly relationship for years, chill out. If they are exes, you may have more reason to ask your partner to set some boundaries out of respect for your budding relationship.

As the two of you do things together, you'll meet new friends who don't "belong" to either one of you, and they are valuable as well. Many couples enjoy spending time with other couples, and this can enhance your time together. Be considerate if some of your "couple friends" were also friends when you were with a former partner; this arrangement may make your new partner feel like the odd person out. In fact, be sensitive about including your partner in conversations with any friends that include reminiscing about events before your relationship started. No one likes feeling excluded from a private conversation. So if you're talking about a hilarious experience from the past you shared with your friends, give enough context so that your partner can participate and enjoy the story.

Considering Religion and Spirituality

If participation in a faith community is important to you, you will most likely want to find a partner with compatible beliefs and practices. If you have strongly held spiritual convictions, consider whether you will be comfortable with someone who differs greatly in this regard. Certainly there are many successful interfaith couples, and you may not care whether your partner is part of a different congregation, or none at all. It's worth thinking about how you might resolve any differences in traditions and religious observance, and talking these issues through with a potential partner early in the relationship if they are vital to your happiness.

Ten Questions to Deepen Your Relationship

Online dating has the advantage of letting you ask questions of a potential partner before you meet. Regardless of how you meet, once a relationship is underway, you may begin to realize how much you don't know about your partner. Certainly spending time together and watching how a person acts gives you valuable information to help you decide if you want a committed relationship. But as your love affair unfolds, you can use gentle questioning to learn more about your partner's core values and to help you decide if this relationship is truly what you have wished for.

When you ask your partner questions, be careful not to sound like an interrogator or a job interviewer: "What would you say are your strengths and weaknesses?" Ugh. Questions can be a great form of communication if you keep your tone gentle, listen attentively to the answer (without interrupting), and respond in a way that invites more sharing. It's also important to balance asking questions with being open about your own thoughts, ideas, and values.

Choose a relaxed time and place for these conversations, preferably when you won't be interrupted. Don't ask all 10 questions at once – that may feel overwhelming! Just work them into the time you spend together. Certainly you can develop your own questions about anything that's particularly important to you. For example, if you have children, you might want to ask about your partner's parenting values. If travel is your favorite pastime, you could ask about your partner's best and worst travel experiences. Just don't hesitate to have in-depth conversations about what's important in life to each of you. How else can you decide whether this is a durable relationship that will bring you both happiness?

Here are 10 questions that may help you get to know each other better. Before you ask each question, imagine your partner's response. Even if you think you know what it will be, you may be surprised. Try it and see!

1. What do you want your life to look like in five years?
2. Who do you respect and admire, and why?
3. Who are the people you feel closest to?
4. What is something you feel really proud of?
5. If you won the lottery, what would you do with the money? (Extra points for saying, "I'd share it with you!")
6. What do you wish you had done differently in previous relationships?
7. What helps you to cope with tough situations?
8. When two people live together, how should they divide up the work of running a household?
9. What do you think about people who don't believe fidelity is important?
10. What makes a really good, satisfying day for you?

SECTION FOUR: UPGRADE YOUR DRIVING SKILLS

SECTION FOUR: UPGRADE YOUR DRIVING SKILLS

Chapter 8: Communication

> But I'm just a soul whose intentions are good
> Oh Lord, please don't let me be misunderstood.
> – The Animals, "Don't Let Me Be Misunderstood"

Introvert or Extrovert?

Jennifer is a psychologist; Charles is a former information technology professional. Can you guess who is the extrovert, and who is the introvert? Extroverts gain energy from interacting with other people, and usually like to process information with others. Introverts generally gain energy from quiet time spent alone, and usually like to work things out themselves before sharing with others.

When we meet our partner in midlife, we are more likely to be thoughtful about our communication process, especially if we have experienced poor communication in previous relationships. When you're committed to a lasting relationship, it is worth taking the time and effort to learn about your own personality style and that of your partner.

Most of us know our own styles reasonably well, but we don't always think to convey that information clearly to our partners. When an introvert and an extrovert get together, it's really helpful to take some time to share how each person prefers to get information, make decisions, and spend time.

Here are a few tips that we have discovered to be helpful.

For the extrovert:

- ♥ Let your partner know that when you say something, you are not wedded to that idea. You're just letting it float by, and you may well change your mind.

- ♥ Give your partner time to process information before pressing for a decision. If nothing is on fire, you can usually wait a couple of hours or a couple of days for your partner to think things through.

- ♥ Find some other people to hang out with. Your introverted partner will probably not want to socialize as much as you do, so make sure you are okay with going to social events on your own or with a friend.

- ♥ If you want to know what your partner thinks, you are probably going to have to ask. Then remember to pause and breathe so you can hear the response before you contribute your next idea.

For the introvert:

- ♥ Let your partner know that you are mulling something over, instead of tuning him or her out. Just say, "I'm glad you brought that up. Let me have some time to think about it, and let's talk about it after supper." Then remember it is your responsibility to circle back to the topic as promised.

- ♥ Help your partner understand that time alone nourishes you, and it is not a rejection of your relationship when you want to do something on your own.

- ♥ Realize that your partner will probably need time with others.

- ♥ Your partner will sometimes want to run ideas by you and work them out by talking. If you are not ready to offer your own ideas, say so and focus on being a good listener.

- ♥ Don't assume your partner's behavior means the same thing as it would if you acted that way.

TRAVELERS' TALES

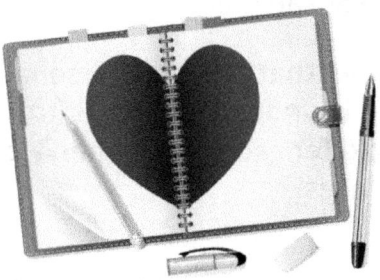

Extroverted Joanne is sure that her partner Frank is angry at her because he has hardly spoken all evening. In fact, introverted Frank is simply contemplating a work-related dilemma, and isn't the slightest bit angry at Joanne. He is so focused on his own thoughts that he has barely registered her presence. When she blows up at him for ignoring her, he is completely surprised. The ensuing argument could possibly have been avoided if Joanne had said, "I notice you are very quiet this evening. Is something on your mind?"

Frank often avoids bringing up his concerns because, in his view, Joanne wants to "talk it to death" and he's often not ready to do that. He could communicate effectively by saying, "Yes, I'm just thinking through a situation at work. I'll be glad to talk about it with you later on, but right now I just need some time to think it through. It's nothing terrible, but I need to chew on it a bit. Okay?" If Frank can take a break for a few minutes and give Joanne a smile and a kiss, she is more likely to feel comfortable with his having the time and space he needs.

If you are interested in learning more about personality styles, you may enjoy reading *I'm Not Crazy, I'm Just Not You: The Real Meaning of the Sixteen Personality Types* by Roger Pearman and

Sarah Albritton or *Quiet: The Power of Introverts in a World That Can't Stop Talking* by Susan Cain.

Above all, remember that neither personality style is "better" than the other. We have learned that introverts and extroverts have a great deal to offer each other when we can respect and appreciate our differences.

Keep Your Communication Skills in Tune

We can all use a tune-up on our communication skills as we build close relationships. Often at the beginning of a relationship, we are sweeter than sugar, but as time goes on, it's easy to lapse into irritability and unpleasantness when conflict arises.

TRAVELERS' TALES

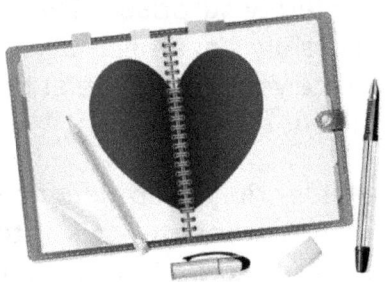

Mario and Janet have been together for three years, and their arguments are getting increasingly bitter. Lately, they have been arguing about Janet staying at work well into the evening every day. Her schedule means most of the household responsibilities, including the care of her children and his, are left up to Mario. Mario gets loud when he is angry, and Janet clams up.

Both of them have been divorced and have bad memories of verbal fights. Neither wants the relationship to fail. Mario has an Employee Assistance Program at work that offers a few sessions of free, confidential counseling to employees. He and Janet agree to see a counselor.

The counselor has Mario and Janet practice identifying their feelings, stating their concerns in a neutral way, and asking for what they want. For example, instead of accusing Janet of being selfish and not caring about the house and the children, Mario learns to lower his voice and speak more calmly. He explains to Janet that he's feeling resentful and frustrated, because he believes he has an unfair burden of housework and child care after his own demanding day at work. Instead of avoiding the problem, which makes Mario even more agitated, Janet learns to stick with the conversation long enough to explain the pressure she feels at her job and to acknowledge and validate Mario's feelings.

The counselor helps them to consider alternatives and to remember they are on the same team. Janet is able to rearrange some work responsibilities so that she can begin working shorter hours in a month or so. Mario agrees that he will shoulder the additional home duties for that period of time, and they agree to hire a babysitter one night each week so Mario can go out with some buddies.

Communication Basics

- ♥ Conflict is not a bad thing. Nastiness is. Work on assertive communication, which means expressing your feelings, describing your concerns as objectively as possible, and asking directly for what you need.

- ♥ Reassure your partner that you value their opinion, even if you disagree. Make sure you mean it.

- ♥ Create a "safe zone" for communication. No one is going to open up to you if you belittle them or have a fit every time you dislike what they say.

- ♥ If your partner speaks to you in an abusive or demeaning manner, or is physically abusive, seek help on your own from a counselor or an advocacy agency (such as a domestic violence program). Couples counseling may not be safe or appropriate if you are feeling frightened.

- ♥ Refer to "Tune Up Your Communication Skills" in Chapter 2. You'll find a quiz to help you identify your communication style and some tips on more effective conflict resolution.

Breaking the Silence

How many worries or concerns are you holding inside yourself instead of sharing them with your partner? Has the "baggage" of previous relationships made it difficult to have the kind of open communication that you know is important?

"The Sound of Silence," as Simon and Garfunkel so aptly put it, starts in childhood. "If you don't have anything nice to say, don't say anything at all." "Children should be seen and not heard." (Parents may not say that anymore, but they certainly did when we were growing up.) Boys are told to "man up," not to cry, and not to talk about feelings—except perhaps for anger. Very few of us came from families where we were encouraged to speak up when we were sad or angry or scared. Our parents may even have tried to make us feel better by saying, "Oh, you aren't really scared (or mad or sad)."

In some families, the silence was deeper and heavier. You certainly didn't talk about it if your dad drank or hit your mom, if a grown-up touched you sexually, or if you thought you might be gay or lesbian, unless your family was extraordinary for the times.

If the romantic relationships you had as a younger adult were not healthy and strong, the silence probably continued. In the absence of trust and safety, the flame of true communication flickers and dies. If your partner didn't respect your opinions and respond gently and kindly to your concerns, you learned to keep your mouth shut. You may even have learned to lie, just to avoid conflict or ridicule.

Now you are starting a new chapter in your life. You're wishing for a healthy and happy relationship, or perhaps you have already embarked on a promising partnership. Do you speak up when things bother you? Do you create opportunities for your partner to do the same? If you haven't found your special someone yet, work on these skills with your friends and family (but only if it's physically and emotionally safe to do so). If you believe you can't be open because of the way your new partner responds, think long and hard about whether you are with the right person. Someone who cares about you will want to hear what you have to say.

When your partner gathers their courage to talk frankly to you, try your best to say, "It's hard to hear you are angry, but I am so glad you told me." You can also ask for some help when you're struggling: "I sometimes have a hard time talking about things that upset me, and I'd appreciate your listening to what I have to say." The benefit of breaking the silence is greater trust and emotional closeness – and isn't that what you have been longing for?

Chapter 9: What's Sex Got to Do with It?

> I can dig it, he can dig it, she can dig it, we can dig it,
> they can dig it, you can dig it, oh let's dig it.
> Can you dig it, baby?
> –Friends of Distinction, "Grazing in the Grass"

> **Amazing turn-ons:** Admiration, appreciation, consideration, attention, and acceptance
>
> **Surefire turn-offs:** Criticism, humiliation, selfishness, disregard, and anger

Midlife Sex: Complicated but Wonderful!

Younger people may be surprised to learn that sex is still an important part of older folks' lives. A survey by the National Social Life, Health, and Aging Project found that people in their early seventies were having nearly as much sex as those in their late fifties.

The good news about midlife sex is that you can keep on enjoying it as long as you're reasonably healthy. Realistically, it's not going to be exactly like the kind of sex you had in your teens or your twenties, but it can be just as hot and a lot less hassle. On the one hand, you may not have quite the energy or stamina you had earlier in life; on the other hand, you probably have enough experience to know what pleases you and how to please your partner. Unless you have kids (or aging parents) at home, you may have more privacy than you had in your youth. You definitely should be more self-aware, more knowledgeable about the physiology of sex, and less likely to take great sex for granted.

> "I'm more relaxed about sex at 69 than I was when I was younger and married. Also, the fact that there aren't children around helps a lot." – *Magic at Midlife* survey participant

When you first get together with someone who interests you, there are decisions to be made about when and under what circumstances to move the relationship into the sexual arena. And unlike your younger self, you most likely recognize that you have to make those decisions with your brain rather than other parts of your anatomy!

As a person in midlife, you may have some complicated considerations when it comes to sex. You may have "baggage" from previous relationships, you may worry about how potential partners will see you, you may have concerns about how other people in your life will react to your "hooking up," and you may wonder how you'll feel if you decide to be sexually active and then your relationship doesn't work out. In addition, once you are in a committed relationship, you'll want to keep your sex life alive and vibrant, and you may have questions about how you and your partner can sustain a passionate relationship.

The major barrier to an active sex life for women is lack of a partner; for men, performance issues related to aging may get in the way. As people get older, they may need to be more creative and flexible about what they do in bed in order to remain sexually active. One issue that no one should ignore is the rising rate of sexually transmitted infections (STIs), even among those over 65. While unintended pregnancy may no longer be an issue, protection from STIs is critical for many seniors.

There are two essential ingredients for great sex at midlife: love and a sense of humor. With reasonable caution and a willingness to accommodate the changes brought about by aging, adults in midlife and their senior years can have fulfilling sex lives – and a whole lot of fun!

To Do It or Not To Do It?

Terrible Reasons to Have Sex:

1. You are afraid your partner will reject you if you don't have sex soon, whether or not you are ready.
2. You're not sure you remember how to do it.
3. You think someone your age shouldn't have any hesitation about having sex.
4. You are so horny that it completely clouds your judgment.
5. You think a "real man" or a "real woman" should be sexually active, regardless of the circumstances.
6. You are drunk or high and it seems like a good idea.

Great Reasons to Have Sex:

1. You are with a loving partner, you have thought it over and talked it over, and you really want to.
2. Your Horny Inner Teenager and your Rational Adult Self agree that this would be a good thing.
3. As Jennifer's mother once said (surprising and shocking her teenage daughter), "Sex is peachy."

What's Love Got to Do with It?

There really is nothing better than terrific sex with someone you love and who loves you, and most midlife couples have the good sense to be grateful that this delightful activity is a part of their lives. For some people, midlife is the first time they have ever been in a mutually fulfilling sexual relationship. For others, midlife sex rekindles a part of them that they thought might be lost forever.

So what's wrong with random sex? We're not the Sex Police, so if you want to have meaningless sex with people you barely know, be our guest (and for heaven's sake, use protection). However, if that is all you really want, it's unlikely that you would be reading this book. We are both old-fashioned enough to believe that sex in a lasting, loving relationship is worth waiting for. Even in this age of liberation, that concept is still harder for the average man to embrace than the average woman, but we believe that waiting for the "real deal" benefits both men and women.

How Do You Decide If It Is Time to Move Into a Sexual Relationship?

We're assuming that you want sexual activity to be part of a committed, ongoing relationship. In that case, it's better to wait a little longer than to start too soon. Your heart, head, and body need to agree before you move ahead. Can you trust your partner? Is he or she respectful of you in nonsexual ways? If you express a concern, even about something minor, does your partner listen and act accordingly?

TRAVELERS' TALES

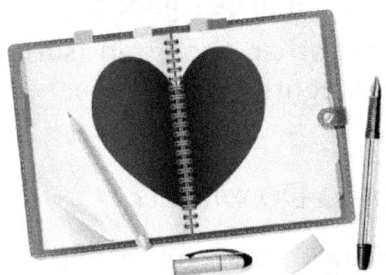

Susan
Susan is an efficient and expert cook, and it bugs her when people stand between the sink and the stove while she is cooking. She has conveyed this pet peeve to Brian several times, but he persists in standing in her way while she's cooking. When she pleasantly asks him to move to the other side of the breakfast bar, he tells her she is being silly and he just wants to keep her company. This isn't such a big

deal, but the fact that he dismisses her expressed preferences gives Susan pause, and makes her wonder what it would be like if this happened in bed!

Jacob

Jacob was widowed after a long-term marriage; his premarital sexual experience included only two other partners. Fidelity and monogamy are very important to him. He has been dating Irene for a couple of months, and she has indicated that his sexual attentions would be welcome. Jacob is attracted to her, but not yet sure whether she is the woman of his dreams. He wonders how he will feel if they become sexually intimate and then the relationship ends. In his view, sexual closeness is part of deep emotional connection. He fears that having sex too early in their relationship will cause confusion in his own mind about whether Irene is truly the right partner for him.

Jacob is very aware of the social expectations for men to be ready for sex whenever it is offered. He worries that Irene will think less of him as a man if he holds back, but at the same time, he doesn't want to feel pressured to move ahead before he's ready. He decides that this issue is important enough to him that he should discuss it openly with Irene. Her understanding and sensitivity about his preferences encourages Jacob to want to move forward at his own pace, and makes him feel emotionally closer to her. He doesn't want to become sexually active until he feels there is a good chance they will be life partners. He understands that there is an emotional risk to becoming intimate if the relationship ultimately doesn't work out, so he wants to make this decision thoughtfully.

Juanita

Juanita is an attractive 48-year-old who has been divorced for three years. She is beginning to feel that if she doesn't find a partner soon, she may have to spend the rest of her life alone. The men she dates are sometimes pushy when it comes to wanting sex, and so far she has turned them all down. Now, however, Juanita is starting to doubt her own attractiveness and to wonder whether she'll ever find someone who is interested in her if she's unwilling to have sex early in their dating relationship. She sometimes thinks that all the men in her age bracket are only attracted to young women, and is beginning to believe that she needs to consent to sex in order to maintain the attention of a potential partner.

One day, as Juanita is thinking about this situation, she realizes that this is the adult equivalent of her experience as a teenager, when she felt she had to "put out" to keep a boyfriend interested. Her older, wiser self recognizes that she no longer wants to be in that position and her self-respect demands that she postpone sexual activity until she has found the right partner and is ready for that level of intimacy. Surprisingly, once Juanita has made that decision, she finds that men in whom she is interested are more attracted to her, because she comes across as more self-assured. Once she talks openly about her desire to wait for sexual activity, she feels more relaxed and enjoys flirting without fear that her actions will be misinterpreted.

Mature Adult Sex Ed

Midlife adults can feel like bumbling adolescents when it comes to having conversations about sex. Most of us weren't raised in households where we had frank discussions of sexual issues. Few people in the "boomer" generation had truly informative sex education classes in school. And because men, in particular, are socialized to believe that they should already know everything there is to know about sex, it's difficult for them to ask questions. Men are also less likely to be exposed to magazine articles about sex (other than *Penthouse* fantasies), whereas women's magazines sometimes seem to be highly explicit instruction manuals.

> "We compromise and try to find a balance of happiness since we have some differences."
> –*Magic at Midlife* survey participant

So what do you really need to know? If you're a heterosexual man, here are a few of the high points:

1. News flash! Women are different from men. Their arousal patterns are different, it may take them longer to reach orgasm, and intercourse alone may not bring them to a peak.
2. Foreplay is a misnomer. Sex isn't just about the insertion of a penis into a vagina. Sex starts when you raise your eyebrow and smile at your partner in an inviting manner. Take your time, and enjoy each course of this meal. No fast food, please!
3. It's amazing how many men don't really understand female anatomy. No one ever mentions the clitoris in sex ed class. Educate yourself.
4. While you may enjoy sex when you are stressed or even angry, few women find this pleasurable.

For straight women, there are some important things to keep in mind as well:

1. It's not uncommon for older men to have some problems achieving or maintaining an erection. This may be due to medications, physical ailments, or a variety of other causes. It's not a reflection of his attraction to you. See the

section below on performance issues.

2. Midlife is a great time to get acquainted with your own sexuality, if you haven't before now. Some women have never focused on their own sexual likes and dislikes and what brings them the greatest satisfaction. You do have to know your own body before you can explain your preferences to your partner.
3. Sex with a mature man may require a bit more understanding and effort, but it can be the best sex of your life!
4. Read your women's magazines – but just take it all with a grain of salt. You don't have to be the courtesan of the century to have a great time in bed.

Staying Healthy to Stay Sexy

The recent National Survey of Sexual Health and Behavior makes it clear that many older Americans are still enjoying active sex lives. However, there are some physical changes that require adjustments in sexual expectations and behaviors over time.

With regard to male sexuality, older men often require more direct stimulation and more time to achieve an erection and an orgasm. Even in early midlife, men will find they need more time between sexual episodes than in their youth.

Women may find their sexual responses changing as they approach and go through menopause. Lack of vaginal lubrication is a common issue, and can be easily solved with an over-the-counter lubricant. Experiment until you find one that both of you like, since lubricants vary in scent and texture.

> "Sex – menopause and drying up. Him – heart problems and medicine making it hard to get an erection. Be open and honest, try different things, find out what you are both comfortable with, talk to your doctor, get informed." –*Magic at Midlife* survey participant

For both men and women, general health and mental health affect desire and performance. If you feel lousy, it's hard to feel sexy. There are no easy solutions to these issues, but there are some key approaches:

- ♥ Talk to your health care provider. If medication side effects or unaddressed medical problems are interfering with sexual satisfaction, you may find relief.

- ♥ Talk to each other. Sometimes a simple back rub may relieve pain so that you can be in the mood for sex. Experiment with positions that accommodate physical limitations and are as comfortable as possible.

  > "A concern: Who has the strongest knees/shoulders to be on top... a problem when both partners have weaknesses." –*Magic at Midlife* survey participant

- ♥ Stay active and positive. Lifestyle changes (such as daily exercise) and an optimistic outlook can renew your sex life.

- ♥ Consideration is sexy. If your partner isn't feeling well, offer to help with the usual chores so that he or she can reserve some energy for fun later.

  > "Sex life was absolutely amazing and playful. But then my husband had a heart attack, bypass surgery, and a stroke. It has been a challenge since then, but when you love someone you learn to compensate, adapt, and figure out different ways to have fun with the 'new normal.' Be creative!" –*Magic at Midlife* survey participant

Dealing with Body Self-Consciousness

You are wildly attracted to your partner and you've decided (after mature consideration, of course) that you want to jump each other's bones. But now the worry begins: *What about my weight, my wrinkles, my scars, my sagginess?* Hopefully the chemistry between the two of you is so intense that neither of you is thinking about the other's possible bodily imperfections. Don't let your own self-consciousness spoil your pleasure.

> "I am in middle age and overweight, and do tend to feel less sexually attractive to him – though he assures me that I'm being silly." –*Magic at Midlife* survey participant

Do pay good attention to grooming. If your teeth need care, go to the dentist. Bad breath is not sexy. By all means, buy new underwear. That goes for men as well as women – your raggedy tighty-whities are not your best look.

Recognize that you don't have the perfect body displayed by models and actors, and reconcile yourself to that reality. Also, be sensitive to your partner's possible insecurities. Let your partner know you consider him or her to be adorable, sexy, and hot!

> "Sex life has been easy. I am a runner and confident about my body, and the basis of friendship from my partner means that attraction was more than skin deep." –*Magic at Midlife* survey participant

Privacy and Other People – "Get a Room!"

In the first throes of a new sexual relationship, we all act like teenagers. This is a good thing. There are few experiences in life that can match the explosive joy of being sexually and romantically attracted to someone new.

While you are enjoying the thrill, keep a few things in mind. First, your kids do NOT want to know about your sex life. Ever. If your children are still teenagers, you will embarrass them to death with any reference to your sexuality. Even if your "kids" are adults, they really don't want to know about Mom or Dad's sex life. Trust us.

If you live with other family members, create an oasis in your bedroom. Use music as a sound screen for privacy, and install a lock on the bedroom door. Don't let other family members use your bedroom as a gathering place; it can be very awkward if the only time the door is closed and you and your sweetie are in the room is when you're making love.

Talk to your sweetheart about how comfortable each of you is with displaying affection in public. Your partner's refusal to hold hands may not be a rejection; it may just be that he or she was raised in a family or a culture that rejects this behavior. Also, beware of TMI – too much information. It's tempting to want to tell your friends all about your new and exciting relationship, but it may make them uncomfortable and you may regret it later.

Don't forget to save a special smile and a wink for your lover!

Chapter 10: Let's Talk about Sex

> "Let's talk about sex, baby, let's talk about you and me."
> – Salt-N-Pepa, "Let's Talk About Sex"

It's Good to Talk about Sex

We enjoyed presenting a workshop titled "Sex and Dating After 60" to a wonderful group of "elders" at a senior citizens' center in Seattle. The people in the audience were attentive and lively. We talked together about how, when most of us were growing up, there was very little discussion of sex. Some parents had "the talk" with us, and other parents pretended sex did not exist. Even in those enlightened communities that offered some form of sex education, the messages were mostly "Don't have sex" and "Don't get pregnant." No one talked to us about learning what felt good sexually, figuring out how to pleasure a partner, understanding our sexual orientation, or how our sexuality changes over the lifespan.

It's probably no coincidence that the rate of sexually transmitted infections among seniors is alarming. No one is born knowing how to use a condom, and embarrassment and lack of knowledge can interfere with protection. Fortunately, it's never too late to learn. No matter what your age, you can probably learn something new about sexual anatomy and functioning, once you stop blushing. The ability to speak frankly about sexual matters can be important to your health and your happiness.

In the workshop, we laughed about the fact that many catalogs specializing in products for the older generation–such as wheelchair cushions or medication organizers–also include at least a couple of pages touting vibrators and other sex toys. Older folks are often still quite interested in sex, and they appreciate the opportunity to learn about options for sexual pleasure as they deal with aging.

When an older person does find a sexual partner, it becomes critical that they communicate with each other. At the outset, it's important to clarify whether they both have the same expectations; for example, do both parties intend to have a monogamous relationship? Can they talk about their sexual histories? Do they feel comfortable asking each other to be tested for sexually transmitted infections? Do they know that a person should be tested for HIV (the AIDS virus) every three months if they are at risk of exposure? Have they ever heard of a dental dam (a thin barrier that can be used to cover a woman's genitals during oral sex, thus protecting her partner from possible sexually transmitted infections)? Do they feel comfortable saying what they like, what grosses them out, and what they're willing to try? Can they be playful while still being crystal clear about what they do and don't want to do?

In a caring relationship, you should be able to freely say yes or no to any sexual act, without worrying that your partner will become angry or abusive or will reject you completely. This holds true for both men and women. Of course, it is helpful to talk about your preferences before you become romantically involved. While many older people are quite interested in sex, others find it unimportant or even distasteful. Being on the same page with regard to your general level of interest and your preferences makes it less likely that either of you will be disappointed or hurt because of differing expectations.

If you still find it difficult to discuss sexual issues, try reading as much as you can and writing out some of your concerns. You can even write yourself a "script" for discussing such potentially difficult topics as requesting that your partner be tested for sexually transmitted infections, insisting on condom use (remember, you can buy condoms yourself, ladies), expressing sexual preferences, or telling your partner (tactfully) that you don't care for a particular aspect of sex. It may also help to begin by letting your partner know that this topic is challenging for you, and you would appreciate patience and support as you try to express yourself.

> "We laughed a lot. We were patient with each other. We tried to overcome shyness with kindness. Now that we are no longer able to make love, we use touch and deep understanding to help us through the loss of this important facet of intimacy. We grieve for what we have lost." –*Magic at Midlife* survey participant

The reward for good communication about sex is often a more enjoyable sex life. That's worth the effort. So let's talk about sex!

Having the "Senior Safer Sex" Conversation

As an older person, you are likely to have lots of relationship smarts – and you still may feel awkward or embarrassed to talk about safer sex with a partner before you actually have sex. Older folks have rapidly increasing rates of sexually transmitted infections – chlamydia and syphilis rates for people over 55 have increased more than 50 percent in recent years. You may also be surprised to learn that a quarter of people living with HIV/AIDS are over the age of 50.

So if you're asking yourself, *Do I really have to have this conversation?* the answer is yes, you do. While some discomfort may be inevitable, if you really dread talking to your partner, ask yourself why. Is it possible that you haven't yet built up a trusting relationship, and perhaps it would be a good idea to wait a while to have sex? Are you just out of practice? Are you worried that the other person will think you're being too forward?

If you are ready to have this conversation, do a little planning. Find a time and place where you'll have privacy and aren't likely to be interrupted. You might say, "Things seem to be heating up between the two of us, and I'm really glad about that. Before we consider having sex, I'd like to talk a little about how we'll make sure we can both be safe and healthy." If you are a man, you can say, "I want to reassure you that I wouldn't consider having sex without a condom. I just think that's a really important step for protecting us both, even though pregnancy isn't an issue." (Note:

Pregnancy may still be an issue if the woman is not completely through menopause, so talk about this as well.) A woman with a male partner might say, "It is important to me that you wear a condom. Is that what you were expecting to do?"

Condoms are a necessity, but they are not the whole story. Don't forget that you will need to protect yourself during oral sex as well (you can look up information online about how to do this). It would be smart for you and your partner to get tested for sexually transmitted infections. You can find a place to get tested by entering your zip code at this website: http://hivtest.cdc.gov. Suggest going together and showing each other your results. Remember that even after a negative test, you will still need to use protection, and that it takes a while for positive results to show up after exposure.

It is sad but true that people who are uninformed, selfish, or stubborn may refuse to use safer sex strategies. If your ultimate goal is a committed relationship, a partner's refusal to consider your preferences, your health, and your well-being is a reliable indicator that you ought to consider looking elsewhere for a loving mate. If your partner makes you feel unsafe or coerces you in any way, this is a warning sign of serious trouble.

In a good relationship, you ought to be able to talk freely, laugh a little, help each other out, and protect yourself and each other. Safer sex will be one of the benefits.

How Can You Talk about the Awkward Stuff?

You could die if you don't learn how to have a candid conversation about sex and risk factors. It's as simple as that. According to the Centers for Disease Control, nearly 28 percent of new HIV cases occur because of heterosexual contact. The rate of new HIV diagnoses in adults ages 40-50 is equivalent to that of younger adults, and older adults are less likely to use condoms with new sex partners. Gonorrhea, chlamydia, and even syphilis are epidemic in this country, and seniors are not immune by any means.

> "Communication is the key."
> —*Magic at Midlife* survey participant

You could also get pregnant, if you're a woman who hasn't completed the process of menopause. It's possible to get pregnant even after it seems that periods have stopped for good. Most 45-year-old women don't really want a "little surprise." So you have to think about protection from sexually transmitted infections and, under some circumstances, pregnancy prevention.

When Jennifer was a college counselor, she asked a young female client who was involved in a casual sexual relationship whether she was using any kind of protection. The young woman replied, "No, I don't really know him well enough to talk about that kind of stuff." Older folks sometimes do just as poorly in the safer sex communication department.

How do you bring up the topic? When you're seriously thinking about becoming sexually active with a partner, you just have to ask. You might say, "I've been tested for HIV and sexually transmitted infections recently. How about you?" Or say, "Before we even consider getting together sexually, I'd like us both to get tested." Don't forget that a negative test result doesn't remove the need to use a condom; recent exposure won't show up, but the person can still be infectious.

Go online, to your doctor, or to your local health department and get reliable information about sexual acts that require protection (don't forget oral sex, for example) and how to protect yourself and your partner. Your life and your health are at stake.

You may want to have another candid conversation with a potential bedmate. It's what we call the "No-No List." With humor and frankness, talk together about what activities are off-limits as far as you're concerned. If the thought of anal sex makes you ill or you find even mild S&M such as spanking to be a big turn-off, let your partner know before you have any unpleasant surprises. Likewise, if you've always wanted to try something, talk about that too.

A brief caution about sexting is in order. Sexting is sending sexually explicit messages or photos by text message or online. A surprising number of adults "sext," and it is certainly their right to do so. However, do bear in mind that once something is sent into cyberspace, it can go anywhere and you have no further control. How would you feel if your ex-partner circulated that sweet nude picture you took of yourself for their eyes only?

Trash from the Past (Childhood and Previous Relationships)

The sad truth is that a substantial number of the people reading this book have been sexually victimized in childhood. Statistics indicate that one in four girls and one in six boys has been sexually abused by the age of 18.

If sexual abuse is part of your past, you can still have a positive, fulfilling adult sex life. You may have some obstacles to conquer first, however. It is normal to have long-lasting effects from this kind of trauma; the aftermath may include issues with trust, intimacy, body image, substance abuse, depression, and sexual expression.

If you are still filled with shame or pain about your childhood victimization, please consider seeing a therapist who specializes in these issues. Another option is to talk with a community-based advocate or join an adult survivors' support group run by a sexual assault center in your area (you can find a nearby center online at https.rainn.org). There is help for both men and women through these free, confidential programs.

In addition to childhood abuse, many women have been physically or sexually assaulted as adults. Unfortunately, physical and sexual violence most often happens in intimate relationships, and often women don't realize at the time that they are being abused.

While men are less frequently victimized in these ways, it does happen, and more often, they may have experienced emotional abuse by a partner who degraded them.

TRAVELERS' TALES

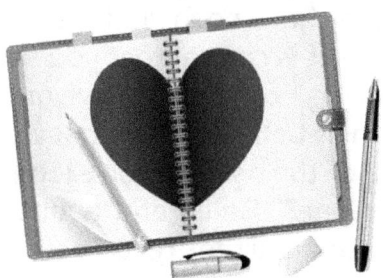

Juliet grew up with a dad who was an alcoholic and had unpredictable fits of violent rage. Before she turned 20, she married Alex, a charming older man who seemed perfect at the time. Shortly after they married, he became increasingly controlling and demanding. His drinking and recreational drug use escalated. Soon their arguments were punctuated by Alex's pushing and shoving Juliet. When she refused his sexual advances because she was hurt and angry, he physically forced himself on her. Her doctor suspected what was going on and convinced her to call a local victim advocacy center where she was able to get help. Eventually, she decided to leave Alex.

After her divorce, she waited nearly 10 years before getting involved in a serious relationship with Paul. When Paul wanted to have sex but she did not, Juliet didn't feel comfortable to let him know she wasn't in the mood. When she and Paul finally talked about her past experiences, he let her know that he didn't ever want her to feel pressured about having sex. They worked out a plan for Juliet to be the one to initiate sexual activity – and to her surprise, she found this reawakened her pleasure in sex.

In an emotionally intimate relationship, partners should be able to open up about prior abuse or other victimization. This can be particularly difficult for men, who fear that they will be judged as less than masculine if they have been victimized. If your partner tells you about past abuse, it is critical that you show compassion and sensitivity. It's amazing how many survivors are re-traumatized by people judging their behavior. Never second-guess someone's actions at the time of the assault–for example, by asking, "Why didn't you tell someone?" Be careful about asking, "Why didn't you just leave?" when a partner reveals a past abusive relationship. When you hear the whole story, you'll be able to understand for yourself why they didn't leave. Some couples counseling with a therapist who is knowledgeable about abuse and trauma may be useful if these issues are interfering with emotional or sexual intimacy for either partner.

Consent and Coercion

During the early stages of dating, in particular, there is a certain element of risk; you can't really know the other person until you have spent substantial amounts of time together. As we discussed in Chapter 5, you have to evaluate the pattern of a potential partner's behavior over time to learn whether the person is trustworthy.

To have a fulfilling sexual relationship, you need to feel safe. If you're worried about how your partner will react when you refuse to engage in a sexual activity, that's not a good sign. You do have to sort out whether your worry is a legitimate reaction to your current partner's signals, or whether it is a legacy from negative experiences in the past. Bear in mind that you always have the right to say no at any time, to any particular act. If you don't enjoy oral sex, don't do it. That might be a deal-breaker for someone who really wants that to be part of their sex life, but if the relationship is strong, you can accommodate each other's preferences.

How do you communicate about whether or not you want to make love? A great technique is the "red light, yellow light, green light" method. Both partners have to understand and agree ahead of time to use this method. If you are absolutely not in the mood, tell your partner, "red light." If you've just been waiting for the right opportunity and you are delighted to be asked, that's a "green light." "Yellow light" means "I might be interested under the right circumstances – convince me!" This is the occasion for giving a tired partner a backrub... you never know what that might lead to! Just be sure you are clear about what you do and don't want.

It's important not to pressure your partner for sex. In midlife, this pressure may well come from the woman, not just the man. Encourage, entice, and invite – don't demand. It's rare that any couple will sustain exactly the same level of sexual interest or desire over time. They can work this out, however, with some understanding and consideration. The partner with the higher degree of desire should become a student of what turns the other person on. If it is soft lighting and good music, go for it! The partner with the lower level of desire needs to be understanding about the frustration that can create. Sometimes you may help yourself get into the mood by creating a relaxing situation or simply opening your mind to the possibility of pleasure. While you shouldn't have sex when you truly don't want it, you might be willing to accommodate your partner by considering sexual activity when you are somewhat ambivalent about the idea.

Menopause and Sex

> "Never underestimate the power of fluctuating hormones. Menopause has been a bitch, but I now feel like I have a functioning body again, and am feeling more alive and interested in and capable of enjoying sex. Having a loving, supportive partner through this time has been very important because we've been able to freely talk about the ups and downs I've felt."
> –*Magic at Midlife* survey participant

Midlife relationships may very well encompass the "menopause years," and menopause can have emotional and physical consequences that affect your sex life. It's important to realize that menopause is different for each individual. One woman may feel mournful that her childbearing years are over, while another may be dancing in the streets because she no longer has to worry about contraception and menstrual hygiene. (Do remember that you can get pregnant until you've gone a full year without a period, and that sexually transmitted infections have no age limit.) In our culture, with its relentless elevation of youthfulness, a woman may feel less attractive or desirable as she ages. Fortunately, there are many older women who celebrate this stage of life and can serve as role models.

Physically, the most common problem that interferes with sex is vaginal dryness. This can be addressed with over-the-counter lubricants or with medications that you can discuss with your health care provider. Taking your time sexually may be helpful, and feeling free to let your partner know if something isn't comfortable is critical. It's best to have those conversations outside of the sexual experience, so you can relax and enjoy yourself in bed.

Sexual desire at this time may wane, or it may skyrocket! If you're troubled by a decrease in desire, the Cleveland Clinic has some suggestions that may help (http://my.clevelandclinic.org/health/diseases_conditions/hic-what-is-perimenopause-menopause-post-menopause/hic_Sex_and_Menopause):

- ♥ "Educate yourself about your anatomy, sexual function, and the normal changes associated with aging, as well as sexual behaviors and responses. This may help you overcome your anxieties about sexual function and performance.

- ♥ "Enhance stimulation through the use of erotic materials (videos or books), masturbation, and changes to sexual routines.

- ♥ "Use distraction techniques to increase relaxation and

eliminate anxiety. These can include erotic or non-erotic fantasies; exercises with intercourse; and music, videos, or television.

- ♥ "Practice non-coital behaviors (physically stimulating activity that does not include intercourse), such as sensual massage. These activities can be used to promote comfort and increase communication between you and your partner.

- ♥ "Minimize any pain you may be experiencing by using sexual positions that allow you to control the depth of penetration. You may also want to take a warm bath before intercourse to help you relax, and use vaginal lubricants to help reduce pain caused by friction."

Women who are going through menopause while they are dating or beginning a new relationship may face some challenges in communicating their needs . But remember, if you can't talk about it, you might not be ready to do it. On the positive side, a new relationship can enhance sexual desire and can be a lovely distraction from hot flashes!

Performance Issues

A young man's biggest performance issue usually is making sex last long enough to satisfy his partner. Older men may have more daunting concerns with achieving and maintaining an erection. It's important to distinguish erectile problems from a lack of desire. A man may be highly aroused, yet unable to sustain an erection. About 5 percent of 40-year-old men have this problem, while 15 to 25 percent of 65-year-old men experience erectile dysfunction, according to the National Kidney and Urologic Diseases Clearinghouse. Erectile dysfunction typically has a physical cause, such as drug side effects, and can often be treated.

It's really tough for a man who has had this problem to approach a new sexual partner. There is no way to know how a particular encounter will go until it happens, and fear and worry about a performance failure can cause that very problem. The best bet for a man with this concern is to choose his partner carefully and to speak openly with her. In a loving relationship, she will do everything possible to help you.

If you're a woman, this can be a difficult situation. Especially if your previous partner wasn't very interested in you sexually (which is highly likely at the end of a failing relationship), a man's performance issues may seem to indicate a lack of interest on his part and may increase your sexual insecurity. The cure for this dilemma is good communication. Both of you need to keep your sense of humor and continue to have frank conversations.

TRAVELERS' TALES

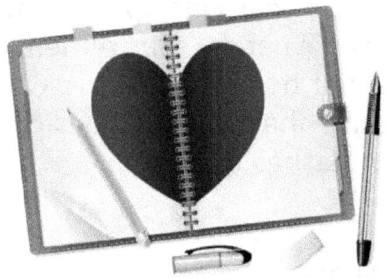

When Joseph asked Alicia about having sex for the first time, he spoke candidly with her about the fact that he'd had some erectile problems in the past. He told her that he was willing to seek medical help if this problem recurred, and that he was very, very attracted to her. Together, they took a playful approach to their sex life. They even found that the erectile problem forced them to have a more varied sexual repertoire, which both of them found highly enjoyable.

Penile-vaginal intercourse is just one activity on

the sexual buffet; motivated couples will discover how to give each other pleasure even without a firm erection. Alicia found that despite her occasional frustrations, the emotional closeness that resulted from their facing this issue together and finding options that pleased both of them created a fulfilling sex life. Joseph was knowledgeable and patient, and Alicia was having fun and great orgasms, so the occasional erectile problem wasn't a big deal.

Keeping Sex Special

The primary sex organ is the brain. Great sex takes place in the context of a loving environment with a partner who makes you feel special. Romance is an essential component of great sex, in our opinion. It's not surprising that the elements of a healthy relationship – respect, playfulness, compassion, and communication – are also the building blocks of a fabulous sex life.

> "Like any other relationship, the initial sex life was extraordinary. However, it waned within two years. Now, the sex itself is extremely satisfying, but considerably less frequent and adventurous." –*Magic at Midlife* survey participant

Take the time to learn what makes your partner feel good, emotionally and sexually. Bear in mind that some people don't enjoy being asked what they like while engaging in sexual activity, because it makes them have to stop and think instead of being "in the moment." If this is the case, find other occasions to have these conversations, and use a playful tone to ask what your partner likes and doesn't like. You can also tell a lot from nonverbal cues and physical reactions, but if you have any doubt, bring the subject up at a later time. If your partner has done something you didn't enjoy, gently ask for what you would like, rather than criticizing their actions.

> "I guess if I have any words of wisdom it would be to try not to get your ego or self-esteem too tied to your ability to function sexually like you did when you were younger. What was once routine and reliable may not be anymore. So, play and love with what you have; don't consider it a second-rate substitution, but a new level of exploration." –*Magic at Midlife* survey participant

Keep the relationship fresh with trips together, an erotic movie that you both like, and a few new ideas to avoid boredom. Stay open to new experiences and keep your overall relationship strong. Older people may have to conserve their energy a bit more than in the past, so don't plan on gardening all day on Saturday if you want to play in the bedroom on Saturday night!

Be aware that pornography is a serious turn-off for some people, and may feel like a rejection. Much heterosexual pornography is disrespectful to women and sometimes promotes violence and disregard for women's reactions. If you are interested in using (nonabusive) pornography or erotica in your relationship, you need to be able to have an honest, respectful conversation with your partner.

Don't forget to enjoy and appreciate your whole physical life together. Spend time cuddling and touching, even if you're not having sex on a particular evening – or at all. Massages, gentle caresses, and kisses should be part of everyday life.

> "This relationship has been the most satisfying I have known. I think my husband also feels this way. Being older, we are more relaxed and interested in each other while less worried about how we are being perceived by the other." –*Magic at Midlife* survey participant

Remember:

Good sex is play, not work.

Emotional intimacy + physical attraction = Great Sex!

Chapter 11: Making It Work

> Life is very short and there's no time
> for fussing and fighting, my friend.
> – The Beatles, "We Can Work It Out"

Exploring New Roles Together

A new relationship is an opportunity to explore new roles. By the time we reach midlife, most of us have had long-term relationships in which we defined our own role, or had it defined for us - by our partner, by society, or by family and friends. Some of us just fell into a role - we did things the way our mother or father did. Or perhaps we actively rejected that model and were determined to forge our own path.

As you head into a committed midlife relationship, take some time to think about who you want to be within that relationship. Do you want to assume a traditional male or female role? Do you expect your partner to do so? (Even in same-sex relationships, partners sometimes find themselves playing out traditional male and female roles.) Our view is that the stereotypical expectations for men and women don't fit most people. Even if you're a woman who loves to cook, for example, you may not want that to be your daily responsibility. Most men welcome a partner who shares the financial load and chooses tasks according to ability - or at least, most men who appeal to potential partners in this day and age feel that way!

Nobody likes to clean the toilet in most households, but someone has to do it. As long as the division of labor feels fair and reasonable, it doesn't really matter who does what. The important thing is that neither partner should feel compelled to take on certain tasks just because they were traditionally male or female duties.

Where midlife couples sometimes stumble, however, is when one partner has a certain expectation that the other is either unaware of, or unwilling to fulfill. If they don't talk it through and come up with something that they can live with, resentment can simmer under the surface of the relationship, emerging as anger and bitterness.

In our family, Charles started out doing the bulk of the lawn mowing and wood splitting, because Jennifer is not as physically able (although she did like to drive the riding mower from time to time!). Jennifer, feminist though she is, did more of the inside work. It just worked out better for us that way.

As it turns out, because of Charles's struggle with Alzheimer's, our responsibilities have shifted; Jennifer is now toting wood and mowing the lawn. It's crucial for older couples to have flexibility and an overlap of roles, because sooner or later, one of you will probably become unable to do what you would normally do. If one partner handles all the finances and the other can't cook a simple meal, what will happen in the case of illness or (inevitably) death?

It's also fun to try out new ways to do things. When Jennifer's parents moved to Florida, her mother made the oven serve as a breadbox - she never turned it on. She said, "I've cooked three meals a day for decades, and I'm done." They ate deli food, went to "early bird" seatings at restaurants, or bought prepared meals. This worked for them!

Midlife is a new opportunity to think about your priorities, how you want to spend your time, what alternatives are available, and what each of you prefers. Maybe it's time to move to a condo if neither of you wants to mow the grass. If you can afford a cleaning service and neither of you likes to clean, go for it. Don't get stuck doing things because that's the way it always was, or that's the assumption you make about your partner's wishes. Talk it out, get creative, and make your life fit who you are now, individually and as a couple.

Supporting Your Partner Emotionally

As grown-ups, we're ultimately responsible for our own emotional states. But the good news is that a loving partner can help us to regulate our feelings and handle stress more appropriately.

Of course, that calls for us to pick a partner who is an emotional adult (see Chapter 6, *Is Your Sweetheart a Grown-up?*) According to psychologist Alice Boyes, PhD, these are the ten crucial questions to ask:

1. Can they make effective repair attempts after an argument?
2. Do they lose control of their actions?
3. Can they persist through frustration?
4. Are they willing to discuss difficult topics?
5. Can they delay gratification?
6. Are they able to admit mistakes or acknowledge their role in a problem?
7. Can they identify "soft emotions" (e.g., feeling sad, lonely, anxious)?
8. Are they self-absorbed?
9. Are they supportive of your successes?
10. Do they know how to boost their own mood?

Assuming both of you rate reasonably high on the positive aspects of emotional self-control, you can each help the other when stress is elevated. The first (and sometimes most difficult) task is to avoid automatic reactions to your partner's emotional state. If your sweetheart is frustrated, anxious, or angry, work on your own composure and self-control. Breathe, take a few minutes by yourself, think of your partner's good qualities, and try hard not to escalate the situation by becoming angry, worried, or frustrated yourself. We know this is easier said than done, but it's worth the attempt.

Second, use humor judiciously. There is a point beyond which humor may not work, but if you can lighten the mood early on, that may help your partner regain a sense of perspective. If levity seems to just make things worse, move on to another strategy. Don't keep insisting, "But I was just joking!"

Third, validate your partner's feelings. We often make the mistake of trying to help someone feel better by telling them why they shouldn't be so angry or upset. "Just relax" is a statement that adds gasoline to the fire of anger and frustration. Instead, ask gentle questions to show you are interested and concerned. Let your partner know that you see their feelings as legitimate, even if you wouldn't feel the same way. Your feelings really aren't relevant if a situation isn't your problem. For example, Martha comes home with steam coming out of her ears because Bill, her supervisor, reassigned a project that was important to her. If her partner George is smart, he won't start telling her to calm down and not be so angry. Instead, he'll listen and say something like, "That had to be frustrating when Bill handed your project off to someone else. You've worked really hard on that project."

Last, wordless comfort may help your partner reestablish emotional balance. A hug can go a long way toward conveying your concern. You don't have to fix your partner's problem – providing a supportive environment is often enough to help a sweetheart regain emotional footing and feel calm enough to work through the difficult situation.

Keep Unpacking Your Emotional Baggage

TRAVELERS' TALES

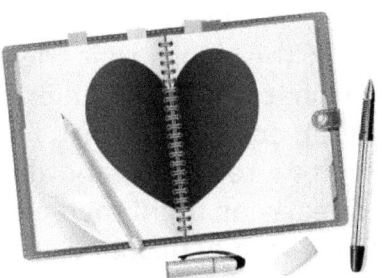

Lakeisha and Andrew have had some rough times lately. Andrew was formerly married to Tanya, whom he describes as very pushy and domineering. Lakeisha's former husband was an addict, who "checked out" when there was conflict. Andrew feels as though Lakeisha is constantly "at him" about doing household repairs; Lakeisha thinks that Andrew is ignoring important home maintenance issues that are just going to get worse.

When they finally sit down and talk this through, Andrew admits that he probably overreacts because of the years he spent feeling underappreciated and nagged by Tanya. Lakeisha realizes that Andrew has a plan to get the home chores done, and isn't ignoring the necessity for them, but he avoids talking about them because he feels pushed. Together, they begin sorting out the facts of the current situation from their leftover feelings from past relationships. Then they are able to start effective problem-solving.

Baggage from past relationships can't simply be unpacked once, and then dismissed. Even when you think you've dealt with issues from the past, they pop up time and again, and may keep surprising you. It only makes sense – we learn how to behave in relationships from our past experience, and we anticipate that our current partners will behave in similar ways to our previous partners.

It helps to be aware of the things that trigger old feelings. You have to differentiate what is a real conflict in your present relationship from what is an echo of the past. For example, Lakeisha found that when Andrew retreated and didn't want to discuss something, she felt nearly as frightened and abandoned as she had when living with her former husband, the addict. Even though intellectually she trusted Andrew to be responsible and to care about her, in her gut she still felt terrified that she would have to deal with everything on her own again.

Working through your feelings is an ongoing process. They won't magically resolve themselves. The good news is that if you have an understanding partner, and you're willing to be honest with yourself, you can have healing experiences that make the past fade away. Lakeisha discovered that if she backed off, Andrew would eventually do what needed to be done. The two of them agreed to a weekly time to discuss household matters and make some simple plans. This helped her to feel less anxious and him to feel less pressured.

SECTION FIVE: ENJOY THE JOURNEY

Chapter 12: Territory and Routines

> Our house is a very, very, very fine house
> with two cats in the yard, life used to be so hard,
> Now everything is easy 'cause of you...
> –Crosby, Stills, Nash & Young, "Our House"

Your Place or Mine? Moving In Together

Half of your partner's clothing is at your place. You are tired of figuring out where you should spend the weekend. Maybe it's time to move in together.

This is a big decision, exciting and a little scary. Knowing when you're emotionally ready to be together 24/7 can be difficult, and it's harder if one of you is ready while the other one is holding back. But let's say you have come to an agreement that it's time to create your own little nest together. Now you have another question: where should we live?

If only one of you has kids still at home or an aging parent living in a mother-in-law suite, you may make the decision based on what will work best for everybody. Sometimes one person is in a tiny studio apartment and the other person has a spacious house, and it just seems to make sense to move to the house. Proximity to work, lifestyle preferences (such as city or country living), and financial considerations may play a big part in deciding where to live as a couple.

Beyond such practical matters, however, there is the issue of territory. When one partner moves into the other's space, it can be a little weird. The migrating partner may feel like a guest or an intruder; the stationary partner may feel disoriented or invaded. These are normal feelings, and have nothing to do with whether you love each other or whether you really want to be together.

Here are some practical tips to ease the transition:

- Take enough time to consider all the options before making the decision about where to live. Encourage your partner to express any misgivings ahead of time, so you can work around them or make another choice.

- If possible, you may want to start fresh in a house or apartment that you move into together. This allows you to start your household on a more even footing and to feel as though it is a shared enterprise.

- If one of you is moving into the home that the other shared with a previous partner, consider switching the master bedroom to another room, redecorating, or buying a new bed (even if the old one is perfectly good). These actions can symbolize a fresh start.

- Make sure each of you has a space of your own, however small. This is particularly important if one of you is a neatnik and the other one is, well, a bit more relaxed.

- A person who is staying in their own home should be willing to give up some furniture or possessions to make room for the other person's things.

- Buy a few things that you choose together, even if they're from the thrift shop, so that the two of you are creating a space that reflects your identity as a couple.

Reimagining Your Life Together

Beginning a new relationship in midlife or beyond provides the perfect opportunity to reconsider how you want to spend the rest of your life. Most of us take some time in our later years to think about how we are living our lives, whether we're satisfied with our circumstances, and what we'd like to accomplish in the time we have left on Earth. Including your partner in this process can lead to some exciting and worthwhile changes.

Do you like where you live? Just because you have "always" lived in a certain place, you don't have to assume you always will. Perhaps your needs or desires have changed. We discovered that we shared a longing to explore life in the Pacific Northwest, rather than staying in Tennessee, where we had lived for a few years. Both of Jennifer's daughters had moved to the Northwest, which created an additional incentive. Three years after we met, we loaded up our household and moved to Washington State, where the natural beauty compensates for the rainy weather! You and your partner may also consider a geographical switch, or you may simply decide it's time to trade your house for a condo or assisted living apartment, move to a new neighborhood, or spend more time traveling together.

Do you like what you do? Whether you are working or retired, are you content with your daily activities? Is it time to change your routine? Do you have a new project you want to focus on? Can you give up the tasks that frustrate or annoy you? Is it time to pay someone to mow the lawn or scrub the bathroom? Is there a creative project you've been longing to work on?

Are your relationships satisfying? Together, you can explore meeting new people or limiting your contact with those who drain your energy and resources. You might focus on a regular time to socialize, either together or separately, or you may want to eliminate some social activities that are no longer enjoyable.

A good way to begin the reimagining process is to mentally step outside of your life; examine the aspects that work well for you and those you do simply out of habit. Another useful strategy is to create a "mission statement" for yourself or for the two of you. What are your most important values and what do you want to achieve? Midlife and your older years should be a time for growth, contemplation, creativity, and enjoyment. If what you are doing is not necessary for survival and doesn't feed your soul, change it. You and your partner have embarked on a new life together; make sure it is the one you truly want.

When One of You Retires

It's likely that one of you will retire (or already has retired) before the other. Most couples plan financially for retirement, but they may not realize that their relationship dynamics may change, as well as their financial status. A little foresight can help to ease the transition.

Talk together about what you anticipate with this change in your family life. If you are the one who is about to retire, what do you expect your daily life to look like? How will your schedule change? Have you communicated your vision to your partner?

TRAVELERS' TALES

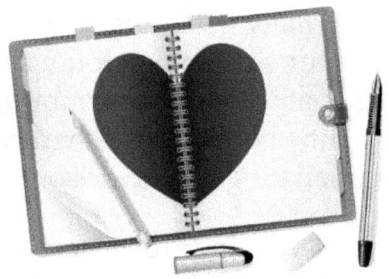

Roy was looking forward to retirement after many years of fast-paced work in a job he no longer enjoyed, but hadn't felt he could leave. For years, he and Celia arose early in the morning, commuted together through horrendous rush-hour traffic, and returned home exhausted and depleted. When people asked him if he had plans for retirement, he would say, "Yes, I just want to relax and hang around the house." Celia was five years younger and felt she needed to stay at her job until her full retirement age. She was accustomed to doing most of the daily housework and cooking, while Roy had spent his weekends doing yard work and laundry.

A few weeks into retirement, Roy was feeling more relaxed than he had in years. He stayed up late doing crossword puzzles and checking his email, and slept in until nine or ten in the morning – luxury! He kept up with his regular chores, spreading them throughout the week. Roy planned several trips for the days when Celia had time off work in the next few months. He was completely surprised when, one Wednesday evening after a tough commute home, the normally even-tempered Celia burst into tears and began shouting at him. After an angry exchange, they both calmed down and began to talk.

It turned out that Celia was feeling burned out and resentful, but also feeling guilty about her reaction to Roy's retirement. She genuinely wanted him to enjoy his hard-earned freedom, but when she scurried out of the house before dawn, fighting traffic on her own while he was still snoring in bed, it galled her. She would arrive home to find him with his feet up, reading the newspaper, while she rushed to put supper on the table. Celia missed the time she and Roy used to spend talking while they rode home from work together. She was also feeling pressured about the travel that Roy was planning, since her idea of a vacation was to hang out at home, visit with her friends, and catch up on her needlepoint hobby.

After several conversations over the next couple of weeks, Roy and Celia realized that they both needed to adjust to their changed circumstances. Roy offered to prepare a simple supper several times a week, so Celia could come home and relax. He made it a point to turn off the TV and make supper a time for them to catch up with each other, and then they cleaned up together. Celia decided she just had to get over her resentment at Roy's sleeping late – he did deserve that retirement perk. They went through the calendar and postponed some of the trips that were planned, allowing Celia some downtime.

Like Roy and Celia, many couples realize they haven't planned for the impact of having one partner retire while the other keeps working. Simply recognizing that there will be unanticipated shifts in your routine and reactions is helpful, because then you can be alert to the need to discuss your own emotions and to be considerate about the effect of this life change on your partner.

Chapter 13: The "M" Word – Do You Wanna Get Married?

> Take my hand, take my whole life too,
> but I can't help falling in love with you.
> – Elvis Presley, "Can't Help Falling in Love"

To Marry or Not?

When Jennifer started living with her first husband in the 1970s (before they got married), she lied to her grandmother, saying she had a female roommate, because Grammy certainly would not have approved of "living in sin." Nowadays, grandma and grandpa are just as likely as young folks to cohabit without being married. In fact, according to the U.S. Census Bureau, the number of cohabiting couples age 50 or older more than doubled between 2000 and 2010.

There are many practical and emotional considerations involved in the decision to marry or not. On the practical side, scores of seniors choose to stay single because of financial concerns. For example, a person who is receiving Social Security or a pension based on a former spouse's employment may be worse off after remarriage. Parents whose kids are still in college may be concerned because financial aid will be based on household income, including that of the new spouse. There are certain tax benefits to being single. Moreover, people with children from a former relationship may worry about possible financial conflicts between their kids and their new spouse.

On the emotional side, marriage may have lost its luster after a bad experience in the past. Some older couples just don't see the point – they're not going to have children together, after all, and getting married doesn't matter in the same way it did when they were younger. The hassle and expense of a wedding may not appeal, and many older couples really don't care what others think about their unwed state. Marriage itself may be distasteful to those who see it as an extension of patriarchy or an oppressive relationship. Until recently, there was a huge contingent of people in same-sex relationships who didn't have the option to marry, because they lived in states that rejected marriage equality.

On the other hand, many seniors do marry or remarry, and find it to be a meaningful acknowledgement of their partnership. They like being able to say "my husband" or "my wife." They prefer to have formal bonds set through marriage, rather than having to draft individualized legal documents with an attorney to protect their financial wishes or other arrangements. Regardless of age, some of us still like the idea of proclaiming commitment through marriage.

The bottom line is that you and your partner should carefully consider, and have frank conversations about, the financial and emotional consequences of marrying vs. living together. Consult an attorney or financial advisor if needed. And don't lie to your grandchildren if you decide to "live in sin"!

Planning Your Wedding

We thoroughly enjoyed our wedding. It was simple, fun, and suited us perfectly. We invited the people we really wanted to be there, we fed them a nice meal, and we involved loved ones in the planning and wedding-day tasks. We didn't break the bank, we weren't overly stressed out, and we had as much fun as our guests–more, actually, since we were each thrilled to be marrying our best friend.

When older couples decide to tie the knot, they come up against all the wedding hype and traditions designed for young folks, which often don't suit them well. The white wedding dress and veil, the big budget, the huge wedding party, and all the drama don't appeal to most older couples.

Here's the easy way to approach planning your wedding. Think of it as two events: a meaningful ceremony and a fabulous party. The ceremony should represent your religious and spiritual beliefs (or lack thereof) and your sincere vows to love and cherish each other. Keep it simple, relevant to who you are as a couple, and sweet. The party should be just plain fun. It won't be fun if you spend more than you can afford, have to mediate nastiness among family members, or are so overstressed by the planning process that your experience is more of a nervous breakdown than a celebration.

The great news is that as an older couple, you're probably way beyond worrying about what other people think. If you want to get married at sunrise in the park or while parachuting out of a plane, go right ahead. If other people won't approve, don't invite them to the ceremony. You need not have attendants unless you want them, you don't have to wear a tuxedo or a white dress, and you don't even have to have clergy officiate. All you need is a marriage license and someone who is legitimately allowed to pronounce you husband and wife (or husband and husband, or wife and wife!).

Talk to your immediate family members (children, grandchildren, siblings, parents, and the like) and find out what role, if any, they would care to play in your wedding ceremony or reception. Children, especially, may feel slighted if they are not included in a meaningful way.

The reception can be as simple as a potluck dinner at your home or as fancy as you please. Music is always a plus, and can come from your sound system, a talented family member, or a professional band. Don't forget student musicians from your local university as a possible source of affordable live music. If you want to save money, serve punch instead of expensive liquor, or just have soft drinks (by our stage in life, there are probably at least a few family members and friends who shouldn't be drinking anyway).

If you're combining households and have way too much stuff anyway, consider letting it be known that you don't need or want gifts. It's not nice to ask for money or to demand that people not give you presents, but you can ask a relative to let people know your preference for no gifts. We told folks that we certainly didn't need or expect anything, but if they cared to give a donation of any size to Heifer International, a charity we both support, that would be lovely. No one seemed offended.

Whatever you do, make sure you each have a clear voice in the wedding planning, that you share the work of preparation, and that you have a wonderful time at your own wedding.

Chapter 14: Money – It's Harder to Talk About Than Sex!

> Even though we ain't got money,
> I'm so in love with you honey.
> –Loggins and Messina, "Danny's Song"
>
> Money honey, if you want to get along with me.
> –sung by Elvis Presley, "Money Honey"

This chapter doesn't purport to be a comprehensive guide to financial management in the later years; it focuses on how partners can work together to create a money management system they can both live with. Communication, compromise, and creativity about financial matters are essential components of a successful relationship. Money is not just a source of sustenance; it represents power, status, security, trust, and survival itself. Older couples may fall anywhere on the spectrum from poverty (nearly 20 percent of seniors are in this category) to extreme wealth, and their concerns range from paying their bills on time to preserving their assets for future generations.

Money and Relationships

It's complicated. Being in a relationship will probably affect your financial status, one way or the other. Some people in midlife wish for a partner to help them shoulder the financial burdens of life, others are fearful of becoming involved because they don't want to jeopardize their hard-won financial stability, and many others simply haven't thought about the impact of a relationship on their finances.

As with other issues in this book, we believe that taking the time to know your own values and concerns will help you to build a stronger relationship.

It's helpful to start by assessing your own "money style." Take this

simple questionnaire:

MIDLIFE MONEY STYLE QUESTIONNAIRE

	Strongly Disagree	Disagree	Not Sure	Agree	Strongly Agree
I don't mind taking risks with money.					
I like to indulge myself, even if I can't quite afford it.					
I make a written budget and stick to it.					
I am not particularly disturbed by being in debt.					
People who aren't financially responsible really bother me.					
I have been exploited financially by a partner or someone else.					
I have never consulted with a financial planner.					
I tend to trust people about money matters.					
I can meet my everyday financial obligations without trouble.					
I have a plan to address any money concerns such as debt or retirement needs.					
I provide financial support to family members, or I intend to do so.					
I am very knowledgeable about financial issues.					
I don't keep good track of my money.					
I have short-term and long-term financial goals.					
I am worried about money for retirement.					
It is hard for me to meet my financial obligations.					
It is important that my partner manages money responsibly.					
I want to keep my finances separate from a partner's.					
The things I own mean a great deal to me.					
I want to leave certain things (money and/or property) to my children or others.					
I am comfortable talking about money.					
I expect to share most financial decisions with a partner.					

Money – One Pot or Separate Accounts?

Couples who get together in their twenties or thirties usually combine their finances, for the most part. For couples who enter a committed relationship later in life, deciding how to handle money can be more complicated – or not. Some couples simply put their income into joint accounts, pay bills and daily expenses from that pot, and work together to set financial goals for the two of them. This may work well, or it may cause more trouble than it is worth.

If you and your partner have widely divergent values about money, financial resources, or financial commitments, joining finances may not be the best option. For example, if one person has a great deal of debt and has not shown a pattern of financial responsibility, it may be wise to defer combining financial arrangements.

In deciding how to handle money, couples may want to consider a variety of factors.

What is your "money style"? Go through the questions in the previous section to learn about your own money style, and ask your partner to do the same. Can you accept your partner's money style? Will it drive you crazy if he or she buys an extravagant item? Will you feel controlled and constrained if you have to accommodate to your partner's wishes?

What do you consider to be fair as far as money goes? For some couples with big differences in income or assets, paying a proportionate share of expenses feels fair.

What is your partner's financial situation? This is where full disclosure is critical. If you are going to merge your finances, you should know your own and your partner's credit scores, and find ways to protect your credit score if your partner's is considerably lower. You will want to openly discuss income, debt (including mortgages), net worth, investments, savings, and accounts. It is probably a good idea to meet with an independent financial planner to go over all of your finances and identify any potential problems.

TRAVELERS' TALES

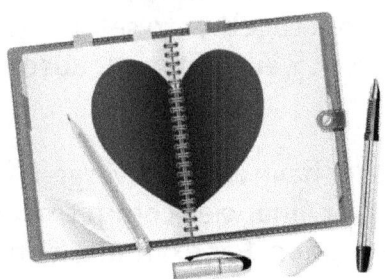

Marianna and Steve

Marianna and Steve met in their mid-fifties and are now living together. Steve is well-to-do and makes about twice as much money as Marianna. She is thrifty and has always managed to live within her restricted means. They don't feel comfortable about putting all their money into "one pot," but sharing expenses equally would place an undue burden on Marianna. They decide to set up a joint account to pay all shared expenses, such as rent and utilities, and each contributes in proportion to their income, with Steve putting in about twice as much as Marianna each month. They each pay for their own personal expenses. Steve occasionally treats the two of them to expensive restaurant meals or other entertainment, while Marianna foots the bill for more modest evenings out. Each feels this is a fair arrangement.

Bud and Taylor

Bud and Taylor, on the other hand, believe that a committed relationship means sharing everything, and they combined their finances after marriage. They took the time to discuss their financial priorities and to work out some compromises. They saw an attorney and made separate provisions for family members in their wills. They sit down together once a month to pay bills, discuss their finances, and make decisions about money matters. Neither of them keeps tabs on where the money comes from – they both consider it "their" money and have an equal say in how it is spent. They have agreed not to spend more than $100 at any one time without talking to the other, so there are no unpleasant surprises when the credit card bill arrives.

There is no right or wrong way to make money decisions in a relationship, as long as both partners feel respected and believe that the arrangement is fair. Money can be a difficult subject to discuss, however, so it is important to set aside time and to pay attention to your partner's values and priorities as well as your own.

Do You Need a Prenuptial Agreement?

Whether to have a prenuptial agreement may be a tough choice. Some people are insulted by the idea itself, but many older individuals and their families feel more secure when they have a legal document that spells out what will happen in the event of a divorce.

Specific advice about these agreements is beyond the scope of this book. Experts do tend to agree that it's important to have separate attorneys if you decide to create an agreement, that you talk through the issues thoroughly with each other and with any affected family members, and that you make sure you completely understand the terms of the agreement.

The Perils of Gift-Giving

Birthdays, special occasions, and holiday gift-giving can be an emotional minefield for people in new relationships. It was simpler when we were younger: we just worried about what we would get and what we were going to give. When you find your partner in midlife, however, you each bring several decades of expectations into the mix. There are extended families to consider, different values and approaches, and the potential for conflict and misunderstanding. Oh boy!

The holiday season can be less fraught with peril if you keep one thing in mind: different doesn't mean wrong. Maybe you hate the commercialization of Christmas and prefer to forego presents altogether. However, your new partner thrives on the thrill of finding just the right gift for dozens of family members and friends, decorates the house like a department store, and wears a Santa hat from Thanksgiving to New Year's. Or maybe you have different religious traditions, and the other person's celebrations seem very foreign to you. The differences could be something as simple as conflict over when to open presents - Christmas Eve or the next morning? Regardless, if you are absolutely sure that your way is the only way to celebrate the holidays, you're likely to encounter friction as you and your partner try to enjoy the season together.

Do you share your finances? If so, you'll have to compromise on a budget and the lavishness of the gifts. One of you may be accustomed to spending several hundred dollars on gifts for the grandkids, while the other considers that a foolish waste and prefers to give small presents or to participate in a family gift exchange. The key here is mutual respect and discretion. If you don't combine your finances, and your partner hasn't solicited your advice, you would be wise to just keep your mouth shut. You may think that giving a 16-year-old a car for Hanukkah is the most ridiculous thing you have ever heard, but it is not your call.

Don't go overboard yourself by showering your sweetheart's family with overly expensive presents. This may make you look like you're trying to buy their favor. Talk together about what would be appropriate. Don't show up empty-handed to holiday gatherings, either. You can always bring homemade treats or a flowering plant to show your appreciation. Again, communication will help you to do the right thing. You don't want to bring a bottle of wine to the home of a relative who is opposed to the use of alcohol, for example.

When it comes to a gift for your sweetheart, follow your heart and your head. Consider how long you have been together, what you can afford, and what will be most appreciated and enjoyed. Gift-giving is a skill closely tied to your ability to listen to others' likes and dislikes. If your partner tries hard but gets you the ugliest present ever, remember it really is the thought that counts. Focus on building your relationship, improve your hinting skills, and hope that the Ugly Present becomes a humorous family legend in years to come. (Jennifer did get a cheese ball from a close relative for her twenty-first birthday. Her daughters still enjoy that story!)

When You Need an Elder Law Attorney

Whether or not you have decided on a prenuptial agreement, there are situations that call for specialized legal expertise. You may want to change your will and your power of attorney (legal permission to make your financial and health decisions if you are unable to do so) once you're in a committed relationship. If one partner has a chronic illness or begins to develop dementia of any sort, it is critical to talk to an elder law attorney to make provisions for care in the future, while preserving your assets to the extent possible. This is important even (and maybe especially) if you are not wealthy. An elder law attorney may be best qualified to help you navigate all the complicated systems that have an impact on your finances if one or the other of you may need long-term care. The sooner you have this consultation, the better.

The National Academy of Elder Law Attorneys has valuable information on their website, as well as a way to locate an elder law specialist near you, at www.naela.org.

Chapter 15: Blending Families – Yours, Mine, and Ours

> Every new beginning comes from some other beginning's end.
> –Semisonic, "Closing Time"

If You Still Have Kids at Home

Integrating your existing family with your new relationship can be a challenge. Here are a few thoughts if you still have children living at home:

- ♥ Be realistic in what you expect between a potential partner and your kids. There probably won't be instant love.

- ♥ If your partner has no children but you do, he or she has to step into an unfamiliar world.

- ♥ Early in the relationship, talk extensively about your parenting styles and expectations.

- ♥ Make sure your partner has individual time with their kids – don't feel threatened by their having some private time together.

- ♥ Work out a good balance between making joint decisions about the kids (especially for issues that affect everyone) and deferring to the actual parent's judgment.

Getting to know and care for your partner's kids can be a wonderful experience, and your partner can be a great influence in your children's lives. However, unresolved issues about kids can also wreck relationships. It might be worth a few sessions with a family therapist if things seem to be veering off-track.

Talk with your partner and recognize that you're going to have to adjust to create a happy family. Try to work out as much as you can early in your relationship, preferably before you decide to live together as a family. Set your bottom-line expectations before you choose your partner. Everyone's happiness is at stake.

If Your Partner Has Kids at Home

Sharing your life with your partner's at-home children can be a significant challenge. In rare instances, you may feel an immediate affinity for the children and slip easily into the role of formal or informal stepparent. More often, there will be a bumpy transition as you adjust to a completely different lifestyle and set of responsibilities, and as the children adjust to having you around.

Realize that building a good relationship with your partner's child or children will take time and effort. Especially at first, defer to your partner for parenting decisions that mostly affect the child, but do address any behaviors that directly affect you. For example, you would be overstepping your boundaries by changing a teenager's curfew, but you should certainly speak up if that same teen left dirty dishes on the couch and you sat in leftover cornflakes.

If you have never had parenting responsibilities, consider taking a parenting class and reading about child development. The more you learn, the more prepared you will be to help build a healthy family environment.

It may be especially important for you to carve out some time alone and some territory inside the home where you can have peace and privacy. Talk to your partner and the kids about this, and help them realize that you are not rejecting family life by taking some time for yourself.

Helping Your Adult Children Accept Your New Partner

Now that you have found someone to love, you're wondering

about the reaction of your grown children. Will they accept the person? Will they be uncomfortable with the idea of their mom or dad in a romantic (and probably sexual) relationship?

We've had some interesting conversations with young people whose parents remarried after the kids reached adulthood. The transition wasn't always easy for the younger generation, but the way in which their parents handled it made a big difference. Here are some tips from these young adults and from older folks whose children and partners seem to enjoy each other.

- ♥ Give your child enough information (but not too much). One young person said that her mother's engagement came as a complete surprise; the daughter had only met the man one time, despite the fact that she and her mother lived near each other. Other adult children become extremely uncomfortable when parents try to use them as romantic confidantes. No matter how old they are, most kids don't want to know about their parents' sexual encounters. This also applies to over-the-top displays of affection when your kids are present. There is nothing wrong with holding hands or the occasional kiss, but anything beyond that may create a serious "ick" factor for your children (and maybe others as well).

- ♥ Don't try to create an instant family. You may think your partner is the most fabulous human being ever, but he or she is still a relative stranger to your kids, in most circumstances. Give them time to get to know one another. Don't refer to your partner's children as if they were your kids' siblings when the young people hardly know each other. Remember that everyone involved is now an adult, and has the right to make their own decisions regarding feelings and spending time together.

- ♥ Your kids may feel a sense of loyalty to their other parent that can interfere with accepting your new partner. Even (or especially) if your former spouse has died, your kids may be conflicted about accepting a new parental figure into the family. And if your children are adults, your partner is not their new mom or dad, and shouldn't be treated as such. In the best possible situation, your children and your partner may become close friends, and the relationship may be something like that with a favorite aunt or uncle. Developing genuine affection and respect will take time.

- ♥ Provide opportunities for the relationship to develop naturally. Don't push, but do try to create situations that allow everyone to get to know each other. For example, working on a project together can create a bond. Charles endeared himself to Jennifer's daughter and her husband by spending several weekends helping them to prepare the nursery before their child was born, lending his building expertise to the project. Jennifer offered medical information and emotional support to Charles's children and they responded with appreciation.

- ♥ Because your new partner is entering an established family comprised of you and your children, he or she needs to be willing to learn your family culture and be respectful of how you and your kids interact (and, of course, you need to do the same regarding your partner's family).

- ♥ No matter how old your child is, talk with your partner about each of your expectations regarding financial support, time spent together, gifts, unacceptable behavior, and other issues that may arise. If you have very different parenting styles and the behavior of any of your kids creates serious concerns, this can endanger your relationship. Ideally, you will have talked through these potential pitfalls before deciding to commit to your partner.

If and when a positive relationship does develop between your kids and your partner, it will certainly make you happy! With some flexibility, mutual respect, patience, and consideration, the people you care about can learn to care about one another.

Step-Grandparenting Can Be Grand

Grandchildren can be one of life's great delights. When you find a partner late in life, you may become a step-grandparent, which can bring great joy and also some challenges. If you have a good relationship with the child's parents and you've been around since the child's birth, your relationship with your step-grandchild may be very much like any grandparenting relationship. Sometimes, however, things are more complicated.

Your stepchild is the "gatekeeper" for your relationship with your step-grandchild, so focus on enhancing that relationship first. Be sure your stepkids know you respect them as parents, and tread lightly with any advice. Offer to help but don't push. Not every parent wants to leave a one-week-old baby to go out, regardless of who is offering to babysit. As we said, in our situation, Charles pitched in to help prepare the nursery for Jennifer's grandson, and has been his beloved "Grandpa Charles" ever since. Jennifer fell in love with each of her step-grandchildren the first day she met them (ranging from 2 hours after birth to age 14), and feels deeply connected to each child. Fortunately, our stepchildren have welcomed the additional grandparent into their children's lives.

Grandparenting shouldn't be a competitive activity. Children benefit from a circle of loving adults. While an occasional pang of jealousy may be normal, don't ever try to demean the biological grandparent or get into a gift-giving competition. The best gift you can give any grandchild is your undivided attention and love. If there are negative feelings between your partner and an "ex" (theirs or yours), walk gently during family celebrations and try to defuse the tension if you can. Grandchildren can sometimes be a bridge to a less conflicted relationship.

Just as parents need to be on the same page in terms of how they handle their kids, so do grandparents. You and your partner will benefit from talking through how you plan to handle holidays, visits, gifts, and contact with all grandchildren in the family. If your partner already has grandchildren when you meet, pay close attention to the nature of that relationship. If you think your partner is overindulgent or too strict, for example, it's unlikely that you can change these behaviors, so consider carefully whether these differing viewpoints will drive you nuts. It's one thing if your partner goes a little overboard for the holidays; it's another if a grandchild with serious problems is living in the home and your partner is in denial about any difficulties.

When differences of opinion arise, the key, as always, is honest and tactful communication. The good news is that co-grandparenting can create a special bond with your partner. You may not have had children together, but each of you can bask in the pleasure of seeing your partner establish a loving relationship with your grandchildren. Together, you can develop creative ways to stay in touch with grandchildren who live far away. You can build new family traditions and wonderful memories as you spend time with all your grandchildren.

Tending Your Relationship as You Tend to Aging Parents

It's your second anniversary, and just as you and your sweetie are about to walk out the door for a romantic dinner date, the phone rings. Your mother's neighbor tells you that your mother has fallen and is on the way to the hospital. The doctor reports your mother will be okay, but she is getting too frail to live on her own. It's only been six months since you and your partner moved in together, and now you're facing a decision about whether to include your mother in your household.

This scenario is not uncommon. According to the National Alliance for Caregiving (caregiving.org), 65.7 million Americans (29 percent of the population) provide care for someone who is ill, disabled, or aged. As we get older, if our parents are still living, we'll probably need to help care for them in some way. This can cause significant stress in relationships, particularly newer partnerships that have begun in midlife.

There is a wide range of caregiving responsibilities, from an occasional respite visit to take care of Dad in another state while your sister goes out of town, to staying informed and involved with a parent's care in an assisted living or nursing facility, to caring for a bedridden parent in your home. Caregiving may include helping with financial obligations, preparing meals, or assisting with daily activities such as bathing and dressing.

Some partners are a tremendous source of help and support to caregivers. In fact, some spouses even take over the primary responsibility for an in-law's care. Others may be resentful or even jealous of the need for a partner to attend to their parent. Even the best-natured partner may find it hard to share your time and attention with an ailing parent, particularly if the need for caregiving is long-term or your parent comes to live with you.

When young couples get together, if they are smart, they discuss whether to have children and how they anticipate handling the responsibilities of a family. Older couples with living parents really need to have the same type of conversations. Topics to discuss as you plan your life together include:

- ♥ What are your current caregiving responsibilities, if any?

- ♥ What is your vision for your level of involvement in caregiving in the future, as your parent's needs change?

- ♥ What do you expect of your partner in this regard?

- ♥ How do each of you feel about having a parent or in-law living in the home with you?

- ♥ What level of financial responsibility do you have for

your parent, and how might that affect your life with your partner?

- ♥ What resources can you access to help with caregiving responsibilities, if necessary?

Caregiving can strain and even fracture a relationship. Clear communication about your needs and expectations, consideration for your partner, and a commitment to find time for each other are crucial elements in keeping your relationship strong while taking care of a parent.

What About "The Ex"?

Most midlife couples have "exes" in their past – ex-spouses, ex-boyfriends, and ex-girlfriends. Even those who have lost a partner to death still have the memories, good and bad, of their life together. For some couples, these memories are the only issues they have to consider with regard to past relationships. For others, the ex is a living, breathing person who is part of their family life in some way.

If either of you still has minor children, their other parent may play a major role in your family life. Relationships with exes can create serious pitfalls in your new love affair. Usually the problems fall at one extreme or the other: you worry about your partner's emotional connection to their ex, or the ex is a pain in the posterior, and you and your partner spend a lot of energy dealing with negativity and interference.

If kids are involved, you have to take the high road. Stepparenting (a role you may have whether or not you are married) can be a treacherous path, although it has its rewards. There are a few principles that can help:

- ♥ Try to stay as neutral as possible, even if your partner and the ex have a huge ongoing feud. Your joining the fray won't help.

- ♥ Keep the kids' interests at the forefront.

- ♥ Never, never, never say mean things about a child's parent in front of the child, no matter how richly deserved they may be.

- ♥ If you can establish a cordial or even friendly relationship with the ex, this may do a lot to ease the entire family's stress levels.

- ♥ Try to keep any jealousy in check. If your partner wanted to be with the ex, he or she would be.

- ♥ Do talk about reasonable boundaries with the ex. Your partner shouldn't be spending every weekend at the ex's place doing household chores while your home is neglected, for example.

- ♥ Be empathetic and respectful about how your new role may affect the ex. It's hard to see someone else living with your children and taking on parenting duties, so do cut the ex some slack in this regard.

While you're in the "courting" phase of your relationship, talk openly with each other about past relationships, highlighting the lessons you have learned for the future rather than the awful characteristics of past partners. The less mystery there is about the past, the easier it will be to trust each other and to understand what may trigger an emotional reaction for your partner.

If either of you has lost a partner to death, special issues may arise. Jennifer, who was widowed after 31 years of marriage, found that Charles's understanding and lack of jealousy about her memories of Mike, her first husband, made life much sweeter. She didn't worry about referring to her life with Mike or sharing pictures and memories. Charles understood that her feelings for Mike were no threat to him or their relationship, and that it was important for Jennifer to be able to express grief when it arose, as it will for any bereaved person. This also made things more comfortable when Jennifer and her daughters wanted to talk about memories of the girls' dad.

Of course, both people have to use common sense, tact, and sensitivity. A house should not be a shrine to a dead partner.

TRAVELERS' TALES

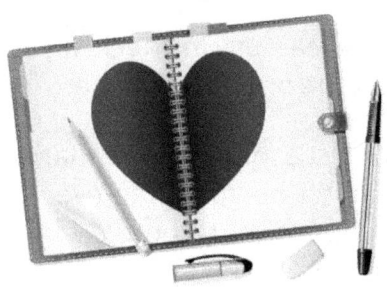

Andrei lost his wife, Olga, after 40 years of marriage. Five years later, he met and married Katrina, who moved into his home. Over the mantel, Andrei had a massive portrait of Olga in her wedding dress. Every room was filled with pictures of the two of them together and knickknacks that Olga had collected. Katrina felt hurt and displaced by the hovering presence of Andrei's dead wife.

Finally, she gathered her courage and spoke calmly and lovingly to Andrei about her feelings, acknowledging his love for Olga and asking if they could work out something that would take both of their needs into account. Andrei agreed to pack up the wedding portrait and gave many of the photos and knickknacks to his children, who were glad to have them. He moved others to one wall of his study. Then he and Katrina began to furnish the house with photos of the two of them and mementoes they gathered together on their vacations. This felt like a balanced approach for each of them: Andrei was able to keep a sense of his history and his love for Olga present in his environment, but the focus was on the new life he and Katrina were creating together.

Living with Pets

Pets are an important part of many older people's lives. As you date and enter into a relationship in midlife or beyond, pets can add to the fun or create (how shall we say this delicately?) a bit of poo. When Charles first visited Jennifer's home, he passed a critical test – her pets liked him! In fact, her three-legged German shepherd, Sheena, enthusiastically approved of him. Charles noticed that the aging dog, who had always been active despite her missing front leg, fell when she was trying to navigate the few steps leading into the house. He immediately put his carpentry skills to good use, building her a couple of ramps to ease her way. How could any woman (or dog) resist that gesture?

That was the good news. Later, when we began to live together, we somehow thought that adopting a Labrador puppy was a good idea. Hah! The puppy was adorable, smart, and loveable, but she was so hyperactive that it seemed she had four pogo sticks for legs. She was far better suited to an active young family than to two older people with busy schedules. Eventually, despite the heartbreak, we gave her to just such a young family, where she is thriving. In the glow of new love and our enthusiasm to add another pet to our newly formed relationship, we weren't very wise in our choice.

Thus we learned the positive and negative effects of "pet parenting" on a midlife relationship. When one person has a strong attachment to their pets, the new partner may face some of the same issues that a stepparent encounters. The pet can be territorial and resentful of a new household member. What is endearing to the pet owner may be incredibly annoying to the new partner. For example, a dog that is used to sharing its owner's bed may growl and snap at the worst possible romantic moments!

We're not sure whether a relationship can succeed if one partner can't imagine life without pets and the other hates animals. This is a fundamental lifestyle difference that would be very difficult to resolve. Even when both people enjoy animals, conflicts can arise. Some simple steps that may help are:

- ♥ Communicate, communicate, communicate. Talk things over – but remember to tread delicately. Criticizing your partner's pet is almost as touchy as criticizing a child. Start with an "I" statement: "I feel uncomfortable when Rover jumps on our guests. Can we figure out a way to help him keep his paws on the ground?"

- ♥ Come up with a fair plan for sharing the workload. If you are stuck cleaning the kitty litter for your partner's cat, resentment may build unless you've agreed to this task.

- ♥ Think carefully before adopting any more pets (hindsight is wonderful!). Will the daily care or the financial responsibility strain your relationship? Is it truly a joint decision? Are you sure the pet is well suited to your lifestyle together, now and for the next couple of decades?

- ♥ Enjoy, laugh, and have fun together with your pets. Pet owning is associated with health benefits and can certainly put smiles on your faces. Sharing the humor (and the chores) can help strengthen your sense of being a family with your new partner.

Chapter 16: In Sickness and in Health

> When darkness comes
> And pain is all around,
> Like a bridge over troubled water
> I will lay me down.
> –Simon & Garfunkel, "Bridge Over Troubled Water"

Encouraging Each Other Toward Wellness

Most of us struggle with our health habits as we get older, and a partner can be either a great help or a significant hindrance. Research has shown that we're more likely to eat in a healthy manner and to exercise regularly if we have an "accountability partner" – and who is handier than your very own sweetheart?

We are often out of sync with our partners – one person starts a rigorous exercise program just as the other one gives up and slinks toward the couch. It is important for motivated partners to offer a gentle invitation rather than a reproachful rebuke, and for struggling partners to be supportive even if they're not yet ready to put on their sneakers.

Here are a few things you can do to encourage each other:

- ♥ Remember that weight can be a significant source of shame, and be kind when addressing your partner's weight challenges. You can't make someone want to lose weight; trying to shame them into it is counterproductive.

- ♥ Set up regular routines that work for both of you, such as taking a walk after supper or first thing in the morning.

- ♥ Plan healthy meals together. If you both like to cook and can take turns providing nutritious fare, that's great. If you are more worried about your partner's weight or health than your partner is, offer to take on more of the meal planning and preparation. If your partner needs to follow a more rigorous diet than you do, be gracious about it and eat your treats when you're away from home.

- Be willing to take on some extra responsibilities to help your partner. You might do the laundry so your partner has time to go to the gym, for example. Don't forget to ask for what you need, if you're the one who could benefit from some accommodation.

- Try to build more activity into your lifestyle. If you are both physically able, you may enjoy hiking, bicycling, or gardening together. Consider a new hobby that will get you moving.

- Plan ahead to avoid pitfalls. Do you have healthy, easy-to-fix ingredients available for nights when both of you are too tired for ambitious cooking? Can you choose a "date night" restaurant that offers healthy options? Do you think about how to stay on the path to wellness when you travel together?

- Don't be the police or a parent. If you tell your partner what to do or what not to do, you're pretty much guaranteeing a defensive or obstinate reaction. Each of us is responsible for our own actions, and an offer to help is more effective than a scolding.

- Focus on the positive, not the negative. Lifestyle and health changes are difficult and it may take many attempts before you reach your goals. Loving partners will remain patient and supportive no matter how long it takes.

- Pick up on the first signs of positive change and give your sweetheart credit for every step in the right direction. Your support and approval can be powerful motivators.

Sickness

As we age, we often develop chronic medical conditions that can affect our life and our relationships. New treatment methods are promising, but most people with chronic pain or chronic illness still have a long road ahead of them. Their partners have challenges on this journey as well.

If you are dating in midlife or as an elder, you may wonder when to disclose that you have diabetes, a heart condition, or any other medical issue that isn't immediately apparent. You certainly don't want or need to describe your health problems on a first date, but don't make them a big secret, either. At the point when you feel comfortable in revealing other personal information (such as the reason for your divorce or the fact that your father is an alcoholic), tell your dating partner the basics about your health condition and its impact on your life. Emphasize the positive ways in which you cope with these challenges. Do pay attention to their verbal and nonverbal response to your disclosure. You're looking for a partner who is considerate without becoming a rescuer.

Once you are in a committed relationship, you and your partner need to work together and communicate clearly about the effects of chronic pain or illness. Not too surprisingly, people who are suffering are sometimes crabby and may be downright miserable to be around. Pain tends to make one self-absorbed, which isn't so great for relationships. It's tough for even the most loving partner to handle the ups and downs of mood and ability that go along with chronic conditions. The consequences of chronic pain or chronic illness may include limitations on a person's ability to work, to travel, to engage in leisure activities, or even to be sexually active. Together, you can develop work-arounds that allow both of you to live life as fully as possible.

To cope effectively with a chronic condition, consider these guidelines:

- ♥ Both partners need to learn as much as possible about the

- condition and ensure that the best possible treatments (both traditional and alternative) are tried.

- ♥ The ill partner can make a true effort to listen, empathize, and support the well partner, so that the relationship isn't a one-way street.

- ♥ As the well partner, you can do everything possible to see things from the other person's perspective and maintain a compassionate outlook. This is much more likely if you have support from others.

- ♥ The well partner also needs to engage in as much self-care as possible under the circumstances. Those in caregiving roles often find that their own health suffers.

- ♥ The ill partner should find creative ways to contribute to the work of the household and the family. Perhaps you can't carry out the trash cans, but you may be able to clean the toilet or pay the bills online. You don't want your partner to have to carry 100 percent of the burden.

- ♥ Cultivate positive topics of conversation and shared interests. Talking about pain and illness all the time is not only depressing, but may even make the perception of pain more acute.

- ♥ Keep your sense of humor and your perspective. Enjoy what you can together.

Memory Loss and Alzheimer's Disease

The last thing we expected when we found each other was that our journey would include Alzheimer's disease. Jennifer was 53 and Charles was 60 when we met, and he was healthy, active, and sharp as a tack. He had gone back to college and earned his bachelor's degree at age 52, and was working in the computer science field.

Over time, we began to notice that Charles was having some memory problems – but then, so was Jennifer and just about everybody we knew over the age of 50. As time went on, we became more and more concerned. Charles was initially diagnosed with mild cognitive impairment (MCI), which we were told might or might not progress to Alzheimer's. Sadly, it has.

We learned that one in nine people over the age of 65 have Alzheimer's, and that more than a third of people 85 and older have this diagnosis. People suffer memory impairment from a variety of causes, including strokes, heart disease, brain injury, and neurological disorders other than Alzheimer's. If you are embarking on a midlife relationship, memory loss from Alzheimer's and other conditions is a very real possibility for either partner. We know this is scary, and that most people don't want to even think about losing their memory, but avoiding the problem won't make it go away.

There are some things you can do to help keep your memory as vital as possible, regardless of whether you have a memory disorder. They are:

- ♥ Physical activity – this has been shown to improve brain health; weight loss is also helpful

- ♥ Social interaction – work, volunteering, and visiting with family and friends are all important

- ♥ Mental challenge – learning a complex skill such as a language or learning to play a musical instrument is helpful; even activities such as crossword puzzles or Sudoku may stimulate the brain

Memory impairment can cause a strain on any relationship, and there are no easy answers. The person with memory loss is often frustrated and may have difficulty communicating even in the earlier stages. The "care partner" (a phrase we learned from the Alzheimer's Association and that we like better than "caregiver") is under immeasurable stress and needs to have robust support systems in place.

There may be some particular complicating factors when memory loss occurs in a midlife relationship. If the care partner's relationship with the partner's children or other family members is not strong, he or she may feel isolated in providing care and support. There are significant financial costs associated with any long-term illness, and this can create stress or family conflict.

It is also important to know that dementia (from Alzheimer's and other causes) is not just about memory loss. Dementia affects all aspects of the brain, and can cause changes in sensory perception, personality and mood, energy, and physical capability.

Both the care partner and the person with memory impairment may feel a strong sense of grief and loss, not only for what they had, but also for what they hoped to have in their life together. Our dreams of walking into the sunset hand-in-hand with our midlife partner must undergo quite a bit of modification. Daily life becomes a challenge, as the capability of the person with memory loss is a moving target. Sometimes care partners underestimate their loved one's ability and they do too much; at other times, they don't realize just how much help their partner needs.

As with any other illness or disability, memory loss is one of those things we must accept as a possibility when we commit to a long-term relationship. We have found some helpful resources:

- ♥ The Alzheimer's Association (www.alz.org) has an amazing range of resources and support, including caregiver support groups. We found that a forum for those with early-stage Alzheimer's was particularly helpful. We were able to learn about issues such as driving safety and to see people who were still capable and productive several years after their diagnosis.

- ♥ Good medical care is a must. Some memory loss is directly related to illness and may be reversible, so a thorough diagnostic process is critical. There is no cure for Alzheimer's, but treatments are available.

- ♥ Participating in a clinical trial, as Charles has, can provide hope and a sense of purpose. As a social worker told us, "Being in a clinical trial makes you feel like you're on the field playing, instead of in the stands just watching."

- ♥ A speech therapist may be able to offer assistance with communication strategies, thereby lessening frustration for both partners.

Our advice is to be honest with others about what is happening. Charles realizes there is no shame in having Alzheimer's, and he has been willing to be direct about his condition with friends and family. This has helped both of us to feel more supported by those who care about us.

Remember what you told your kids: Life is not fair. Nonetheless, it can be rewarding and enjoyable, even under pressure, if you focus on the positive.

Death

Talking about death is seldom easy, and it's probably the last thing you want to think about with regard to your midlife partner. You may have already experienced the death of a partner, one of the most painful possibilities in life. Like many of us, you probably prefer to avoid the subject altogether.

Unfortunately, refusing to talk about death simply makes things harder for those who survive. There are practical matters to be decided and preferences to convey. It's better to make these decisions now, while you can be an active participant, than to expect your partner and family to have to guess at your wishes after you are gone.

Decisions about death can be more complicated when you and your partner start your relationship later in life. Think of all the ugly cases in the media involving a deceased celebrity's adult children and current spouse arguing over money, property, or end-of-life care. Both your partner and your children, if you have any, may feel entitled to be the decision-makers, creating nearly unresolvable conflicts.

So take a deep breath and just do it – talk about death. Sit down with your partner and discuss all the nitty-gritty issues:

- Do you want to be an organ donor?
- Do you wish to be buried or cremated?
- Where do you want to be buried or have your ashes placed?
- What kind of funeral or memorial service do you want, if any?
- Do you have (or need to look into) life insurance and/or long-term care insurance?
- How would either of you manage if the other were to die first?
- Do you have a will, a living will, and a durable power of attorney for health care and financial matters? If so, what do they contain? If not (or if they are not up-to-date), it's time to see a lawyer (possibly an elder law attorney).
- Where are your important papers?

Be aware that these topics can be very emotional. For example, your partner may have always planned to be buried next to their deceased previous spouse, but this plan may hurt you deeply. Your children may be expecting to inherit money or property, but this could leave your partner without adequate resources to live on.

If you have a child who is a health care professional, you may feel more comfortable having them make decisions about your care if it becomes necessary, but this could offend your partner.

Once you and your partner have talked these issues through, be sure to communicate your decisions to your children (preferably in writing, followed by discussion) to lessen the likelihood of nasty conflict among your survivors. Focus on your own wishes, your sense of fairness, and the needs of your partner and family as you consider these important issues.

SECTION SIX: KEEP ON TRUCKIN' – AND SINGIN' TO THE RADIO

SECTION SIX:
KEEP ON TRUCKIN' – AND SINGIN' TO THE RADIO

Chapter 17: Partners on the Road

> What the world needs now is love, sweet love.
> It's the only thing that there's just too little of.
> – Sung by Dionne Warwick,
> "What the World Needs Now Is Love"

Enjoy Your Stories

As you develop a committed relationship, the two of you have some stories to tell. These accounts–how you met and fell in love, how you knew you were right for each other, and how you decided to become a couple–are important. As you begin to shape the story of your life together, you deepen your identity as a couple.

When you first met, you told each other anecdotes about your life. Our individual stories are how we present ourselves to the world; they show what we think of ourselves and others who matter to us. With each shared tale, you began to know each other better and to understand the worldview and the character of the person who would become your partner.

This sharing is especially important for older couples, because so much of the highway of life has already been traversed; learning about each other brings you to the point where you can begin traveling that road together.

Don't get impatient if your partner tells the same story more than once. This may just be a "senior moment," but it also may mean that a different aspect of that story is important right now. Ask questions to enhance your understanding of what happened and how it affected your sweetheart.

The story of the two of you can be a source of joy. Have fun laughing at the humorous events and bringing back the electricity you felt early in your relationship. Use your story (only the G-rated parts!) to help family members and friends understand what drew you together and why you chose to combine your lives.

Be kind and respectful when you tell an anecdote about your partner or the two of you. You may think it's hilarious that your partner's clothing split a seam while the two of you were dancing at your wedding reception, but that may be an embarrassing memory for your spouse. If a tale isn't funny to the person or persons at the center of the story, it's not funny. Stop telling it.

We have found that even strangers enjoy a good love story. So many times, when people learned that we were newlyweds, they would smile and ask about how we got together. They often sought advice on finding a partner in midlife themselves (hence, this book). We enjoy hearing others' experiences as well.

Your shared story is unique and beautiful, and it can shine some sunlight into darker times. Remembering why and how you fell in love can help you to overcome momentary irritations and to focus on the joys of being together.

Lucky to Have You: Gratitude Enhances Relationships

When you find a terrific partner later in life, you are usually smart enough to appreciate how wonderful it is to be with that person. However, as with most things, once the novelty wears off, couples can forget to focus on the positive aspects of their relationship and, instead, get caught up in the small irritations of everyday life. When you make a conscious effort to experience and express gratitude for your partner, you make a major investment in the success of your relationship.

Amy Gordon, PhD, and her colleagues published research under the title "To Have and to Hold: Gratitude Promotes Relationship Maintenance in Intimate Bonds," which demonstrates how gratitude for a partner's behavior and attitudes creates a positive cycle that ultimately leads to happier and more sustainable relationships. When you appreciate what your partner does and who your partner is, your actions tend to promote generosity and comfort for each of you. It's easy to get stuck on the petty annoyances that every couple experiences. If you can redirect your thoughts to how lucky you are to have a loving person in your life and to your partner's positive traits, the whole relationship will benefit.

Terri Orbuch, PhD, a sociology professor, has conducted a long-term research study to determine what enhances the happiness and satisfaction of couples over the years. She says that the happiest couples in her study focused on how grateful they were for their partner's presence in their lives. Not surprisingly, these couples showed humor, empathy, and humility along with gratitude.

Being grateful has benefits for you as an individual as well as for your relationship. Research by Robert Emmons, PhD, professor of psychology at the University of California-Davis, shows that practicing gratitude (by writing in a gratitude journal, for example) enhances people's physical and emotional well-being and helps them progress toward their goals, sometimes to a surprising extent.

So how do you practice gratitude? Take a few moments to think about how lucky you are to be in a loving relationship. Identify some of your favorite things about your partner. Consider writing a little note saying something like, "I am so grateful that you started the car for me on this cold winter morning! I love you." Remember why you fell in love in the first place. And don't forget to say "thank you" for small things your partner does with you in mind.

Chapter 18: Keep Your Sense of Humor and Playfulness

> Let the disappointments pass, let the laughter fill your glass.
> –Jackson Browne, "The Only Child"

Enjoy Life Together

Life is short. Enjoy it together! If you are lucky enough to have a loving partner in midlife, remember to share fun on a regular basis. This keeps your relationship strong and your heart merry.

Even if work demands, health concerns, or other life troubles weigh you down, take a break and do something that is pleasurable together. Aside from the obvious choice (making mad, passionate love, of course), simple activities that are fun for both of you are worth planning. Make a special meal together, have a weekend TV marathon to catch up on episodes of a favorite show, give each other back rubs, take a walk and enjoy the sunset, go to the park with a grandchild or your dog (or both!), or take each other out for an ice cream cone. You don't have to spend a lot of money or even a lot of time to make special memories.

Make the ordinary extraordinary. When you sing along to rock 'n roll on a car trip or add a fun activity to a mundane task, you build a storehouse of good feelings that can help cushion the inevitable frictions of life together. Just remembering to be pleasant and playful as you go about your regular routines can brighten your partner's day. A love note on the coffee pot or bringing home a little treat makes your sweetheart feel loved and special.

There's nothing wrong with having fun with friends or pursuing a hobby alone. But if a week has gone by and the two of you haven't spent quality time together, you may want to shift your priorities. Some busy couples designate a "date night" or have a regular time to be with each other, such as Sunday afternoon. To add a little spice to your time together, you might take turns planning a surprise activity that you're reasonably certain your partner will enjoy. (The other person's responsibility is to be a good sport, even if things don't turn out to be as pleasant as planned.)

Every couple is different. Some folks like to work on projects together, while others might find that to be sheer torment. It's easier if your tastes are fairly similar, but if not, you'll have to work harder to find common ground for enjoyment. It's also kind to occasionally participate in your partner's favorite activities if asked, even if fishing or football or art galleries aren't really your thing. If you will be truly miserable (no horror movies for Jennifer!), find something else you can do together and don't begrudge your partner's indulgence in golf or quilting if it's balanced by time spent with you.

Put your plans for fun on the calendar so they don't get shoved to the side. If time is tight, be creative. Take sandwiches to the park for an impromptu supper picnic, or do the crossword puzzle together before bed. If money is tight, be even more creative. Scour the local paper for free or low-cost activities such as college concerts or hometown parades. Borrow a movie DVD from the library. Take a "stay-cation" by finding new things to do in your own area instead of traveling. Look for discounts on attractions through Groupon, Living Social, or similar sites.

Most of all, remember to put the same enthusiasm and attention into your time together as you did when you were dating. Being fully present and considering the other person is the key to a good time. On a really good date, you try to help your partner enjoy the time with you, listen carefully, find common interests, laugh a lot, and focus on making whatever you do special. Doesn't that still sound like a recipe for fun?

The Couple That Laughs Together, Stays Together

A research study by Bazzini and colleagues (2007) found that couples who reminisced about shared laughter showed more satisfaction with their relationships. Humor helps us to overcome obstacles and increases our emotional resilience, and having fun together certainly makes relationships more enjoyable.

How can you harness the power of humor in your relationship? First, start with revisiting memories of situations in which the two of you laughed and laughed. You'll probably find yourself giggling all over again!

Consider whether either or both of you really need a good laugh when you choose a movie or television show to watch. Some shows that are really "dark" are terrific, but they may not be a good choice when lightening the mood is in order.

Look for humor throughout the day and share your observations with each other. What struck you as really amusing? Just being more aware of funny things can make your day go better, and having someone to share them with is a bonus.

Kids, grandkids, and pets are usually good for a laugh! Share funny pictures, stories, or videos and smile away!

Try to be open to humor even when you don't feel well. There is research showing that laughter can minimize pain and speed rehabilitation (Godfrey, 2004). Focusing on something funny or trying to see the humor in tough situations may ease suffering.

Be careful not to use humor as a weapon. If you are making a joke about someone else, and they don't find it funny, it's not funny. Telling someone they are "too sensitive" because they're offended by humor at their expense is just plain mean. Apologize sincerely and don't do it again. (Sorry for the scolding, but this is a pet peeve for Jennifer, who as a psychologist has heard many people describe the pain caused by offensive humor.)

Do remember to laugh at yourself. We all mess up, and sometimes it's true that you just have to laugh or cry (and we've done both!).

Sharing laughter can bring you closer and build great memories. So tell a joke, watch a funny video or movie, chuckle at your partner's jokes even if they aren't high comedy, and choose laughter whenever you can.

For a little senior humor, here's one of our favorites: a cartoon titled, "Why Dinosaurs Are Extinct." Two dinosaurs are sitting on a rock in the ocean watching Noah's Ark sail off into the distance. One says to the other, "Oh crap, was that today?" It's always funnier when you can relate!

Chapter 19: Share Your Hopes and Dreams

> And in the end, the love you take is
> equal to the love you make.
> –The Beatles, "The End"

Creating Shared Goals

Young couples usually have simple objectives in mind – starting a family, buying a home, and creating a life together. If you met your partner in midlife or later, your relationship can become stronger and more enjoyable through the creation of shared goals that fit your stage of life.

The first step, preferably taken before you start looking for a partner, is to clarify your own goals. This time of life provides a wonderful opportunity to reassess your personal goals and to think about what you want to accomplish. What is most important to you? What do you really care about doing during your time on Earth? Some people find this morbid, but the exercise of writing your own obituary or eulogy can be a useful way to think through how you'd like to be remembered, and what you need to do before your options expire. Have you always wanted to write a novel or compose a symphony? Do you want to focus on strengthening your bonds with children and grandchildren? Will you feel your life is incomplete if you never get to see the Eiffel Tower? (See Chapter 1 for more ideas.)

If nothing else, thinking about your own goals will help as you get to know potential partners. Talking about hopes and dreams is a wonderful way to learn about each other's values and desires. It can bring the conversation to a deeper level and allow you to connect on important issues.

Once you find your special someone, the two of you can enjoy creating a shared vision of the future. While of course we never know what fate has in store for us, holding hands and dreaming together is a joyous part of a new relationship at any age. If you are clear and explicit about your own goals, you can avoid the heartbreak of choosing a partner who can neither join you nor support you. Some compromise may be necessary, but true love does not require abandoning what you hold most dear.

Some goals require agreement: where to live, major financial decisions, inviting other family members to live with you, and more. Some goals simply require that you support each other: giving your partner time and space to write or paint, cheering as your partner runs a marathon, or cooking healthy meals to support your partner's weight loss. Still other goals offer the opportunity to join each other in making this a creative, productive, and enjoyable time of life.

You may find wonderful possibilities together. Exploring new places and passions with a companion can be double the fun, and in the process, the two of you may decide to get your scuba certification, build a house, train a service dog, or plant a garden. Working side-by-side on a project can enhance your bond and your enjoyment of the work. Of course, each of you will still have interests and activities that the other finds boring or distasteful, and that's okay. Each couple has to find the right balance of time together and time alone.

Riding Through Life Together

We'd like to share these final reflections on your journey together.

A loving partner can make all the difference as we navigate life's highways. If you think of life as a journey down the road, progress can be augmented by your skill and determination, but may also be hampered by potholes and strong winds. It is a comfort and a blessing to have a companion on this journey who wants to help you succeed and be happy.

When you find your partner later in life, you most likely have been driving alone for some time. This can enhance your skill; you can manage just fine on your own. However, it is often exhausting. You feel solely responsible for what is happening in your life, and you have only yourself to rely on. Sometimes you wish you could just coast for a while, and let another pair of strong arms handle the wheel. At other times, illness, crisis, or simple loneliness makes it difficult to stay on course, and you long for a little help.

You may have had partners in the past who let you do all the driving, even when they were capable. You may even have had to tow their car, to the point of nearly wrecking your own. You built up your muscles, but also your defenses.

Now you are content to ride side-by-side with your life partner. There are times when you will exert more effort, and times when your partner will, but you know that each of you is giving it your best. You feel most loved when the traffic is horrendous, or the weather makes it hard to see the road ahead, and your partner calmly and gently encourages you, helping out if necessary. Sometimes just having someone give you a little break allows you to settle in, find your own rhythm, and begin to move forward once again.

You would never stand by and watch your partner drive off a cliff; you know that you have the same assurance of support. At times, you each move off to explore a country lane on your own; other times, you set off on an adventure together. Watching the scenery is more exciting when you can share the experience. You work to create your safe haven and welcome each other home. Being together allows each of you to be your best, strongest self, to guide each other through the fog, and to have courage in the face of storms.

Resources and References

Resources

Alzheimer's Disease and Other Dementias

The Alzheimer's Association offers information and support on memory loss and dementia:
 www.alz.org

Caregiving

The National Alliance for Caregiving has resources and information for family caregivers:
 http://www.caregiving.org

Dating Information

The American Association of Retired Persons (AARP) posts up-to-date information on online dating and other topics:
 www.aarp.org

Death and End of Life Issues

End of Life: Helping with Comfort and Care. National Institute on Aging.
 http://www.nia.nih.gov/health/publication/end-life-helping-comfort-and-care/planning-end-life-care-decisions

Funeral Consumers Alliance – This is a nonprofit organization that provides information about burial and planning for death, with resources:
 http://www.funerals.org

Domestic Violence

Information and listings of local domestic violence programs are available through the National Domestic Violence Hotline at 1-800-799-SAFE (7233) or www.thehotline.org. These resources offer a confidential 24/7 response.

HIV Testing

You can find a place to get tested by entering your zip code at this website: http://hivtest.cdc.gov.

Keeping Kids Safe

Darkness to Light (www.d2l.org) is a program to educate parents about the dangers of sexual abuse.

Gavin De Becker's book *Protecting the Gift: Keeping Children and Teenagers Safe (and Parents Sane)* offers a great deal of information about spotting predators.

Boys Town Press publishes a book called *Unmasking Sexual Con Games* in versions for both parents and teens.

Legal Issues

The National Academy of Elder Law Attorneys has valuable information on their website, as well as a way to locate an elder law specialist near you: www.naela.org.

10 Things You Should Know About Writing a Will. AARP.
    http://www.aarp.org/money/estate-planning/info-09-2010/ten_things_you_should_know_about_writing_a_will.html

Personality Styles

I'm Not Crazy, I'm Just Not You: The Real Meaning of the Sixteen Personality Types by Roger Pearman and Sarah Albritton

Quiet: The Power of Introverts in a World That Can't Stop Talking by Susan Cain.

Sexual Assault

You can find Information about recovery from sexual abuse or assault and a local sexual assault program by calling the National Sexual Assault Hotline at 1-800-656-HOPE (4673) or going online to RAINN (Rape, Abuse, and Incest National Network) at https://rainn.org.

Sex

For information on sex and menopause, the Cleveland Clinic has some suggestions that may help:
> http://my.clevelandclinic.org/health/diseases_conditions/hic-what-is-perimenopause-menopause-postmenopause/hic_Sex_and_Menopause

Senior Sex. Medicine.Net
> http://www.medicinenet.com/senior_sex/article.htm

References

Bazzini, D. P., Stack, E.R., Martincin, P.D., & Davis, C.P. (2007). The effect of reminiscing about laughter on relationship satisfaction. *Motivation and Emotion, 31*(1), 25-34.

Boyes, A. Ten Essential Emotion Skills to Look for in a Partner, *Psychology Today*, http://www.psychologytoday.com/blog/in-practice/201304/10-essential-emotion-skills-look-in-partner

Emmons, R. *Gratitude and Well-Being.* http://psychology.ucdavis.edu/research/research-labs/emmons-lab

Godfrey, J. R. (2004). Toward optimal health: The experts discuss therapeutic humor. *Journal of Women's Health, 13*(5), 474-479.

Gordon, A.M., Impet, E.A., Kogan, A., Oveis, C., & Keltner, D. (2012). To have and to hold: gratitude promotes relationship maintenance in intimate bonds. *Journal of Personality and Social Psychology, 103* (2), 257-74.

Orbuch, T.L. *The Early Years of Marriage Project.* University of Michigan, Institute for Social Research. http://projects.isr.umich.edu/eym

www.ingramcontent.com/pod-product-compliance
Lightning Source LLC
LaVergne TN
LVHW051055080426
835508LV00019B/1889